The Wings of
the Morning

Books by George H. Morrison

Highways of the Heart

The Weaving of Glory

Wind on the Heath

The Wings of the Morning

The Morrison Classic Sermon Series

The Wings of the Morning

George H. Morrison

kregel
PUBLICATIONS

Grand Rapids, MI 49501

The Wings of the Morning by George H. Morrison.

Copyright © 1994 by Kregel Publications.

Published in 1994 by Kregel Publications, a division of Kregel, Inc., P.O. Box 2607, Grand Rapids, MI 49501. Kregel Publications provides trusted, biblical publications for Christian growth and service. Your comments and suggestions are valued.

Cover Photograph: POSITIVE IMAGES, Patricia Sgrignoli
Cover and Book Design: Alan G. Hartman

Library of Congress Cataloging-in-Publication Data
Morrison, George H. (George Herbert), 1866–1928.
  The wings of the morning / George H. Morrison.
    p.   cm. (The Morrison Classic Sermon Series)
  Originally published: New York: Hodder and Stoughton.
    1. Sermons, English—Scotland. 2. United Free Church of Scotland—Sermons. 3. Presbyterian Church—Scotland—Sermons. I. Title. II. Series: Morrison, George H. (George Herbert), 1866-1928. The Morrison Classic Sermon Series.
BX9178.M6W55   1994   252'.052—dc20   94-25571
                                                CIP
ISBN 0-8254-3288-x (paperback)

          1 2 3 4 5 Printing / Year 98 97 96 95 94

Printed in the United States of America

Contents

Publisher's Foreword

One wonders if the old wit's comment on sermons applies to sermon books as well when he said that a sermon was something a preacher would travel across the country to give but most people wouldn't walk across the street to hear. The initial response to a book of sermons by a turn-of-the-century Scotsman may be somewhat skeptical—in an era dominated by sophisticated media, savvy marketing analysis, and seeker-sensitive communication models, the pressured pastor might wonder about the benefits of reading "relic" sermons.

It was C. S. Lewis who referred to the historical fallacy of regarding works of the past, particularly the classics and the Bible, as irrelevant and untrustworthy based on the criterion of age alone. His comment—"This mistaken preference for the modern books and this shyness of the old ones is nowhere more rampant than in theology."—applies equally as well to pastoral theology.[1]

Issues of truth ought not to be subject to a statute of limitations, but to paraphrase Thomas Oden, we blithely assume that in preaching—"just as in corn poppers, electric toothbrushes, and automobile

---

1. C. S. Lewis, "On the Reading of Old Books" in *God in the Dock*, ed. Walter Hooper (Grand Rapids: Eerdmans, 1970), 200.

exhaust systems—new is good, newer is better, and newest is best."[2] Morrison's sermons represent, without question, not only a different culture (early twentieth-century Scotland which had more in common with the nineteenth century than with our own era) but also a different pastoral model. If pastors are physicians of the soul, then Morrison's ministry had more in common with the hometown doctor who made housecalls (Morrison was legendary for his visitation ministry, sometimes averaging a thousand calls a year) than the modern medical specialist (and pastor) with his sophisticated array of technology.

Morrison's value, therefore, for the modern pastor-preacher does not lie in his insights into church management, church growth, or contemporary worship. Morrison most likely would have eschewed the whole notion of a "contemporary gospel." What he would have championed today—passionately and patiently—was the relevant and compelling presentation of biblical truth that touches both the intellects and the emotions of contemporary listeners. His value for the modern reader lies in appreciating and learning from a style and sermonic approach that was contemporary in its time and whose principles have enduring value.

What can we learn, then, from Morrison? For one thing, he respected the intelligence of his listeners. His sermons are filled with allusions and quotations from a wide range of literature common to the experience of his people—Burns, Milton, Dickens, and Shakespeare—but without any hint of intellectualism or pedantry. Morrison perfectly prefigures Charles Swindoll's comment that preachers should get a good education and then get over it!

Modern preachers would do well to analyze Morrison's style of literary reference and determine the common cultural mediums of our own day. Lacking a similarly cohesive cultural identity, we may have to search harder for the insightful reference or provide a window for the congregation through which to view another world (consider, for example, the difference between quoting Shakespeare and any current TV commercial). Morrison not only spoke of beautiful truths, but he sought to speak the truth beautifully and for help turned to the great English writers and poets.

Morrison also placed the sermon in a strategic context—the awful carnage of World War I (in which Morrison's own son was

---

2. Thomas Oden, "On Not Whoring After the Spirit of the Age," in *No God But God*, ed. Os Guinness and John Seel (Chicago: Moody Press, 1992), 195.

killed), the emerging discoveries of modern science, or the urbanization of the once predominately rural Scottish society and the corresponding problems of secularization, alienation, and loneliness. Morrison addressed the developing cultural, social, and political dynamics of the day with both challenging and comforting truths from the Word. If we look closely at the changing demographics and family structures in our own society, we will find ample opportunities for strategically-formulated points of reference.

One other obvious characteristic of Morrison's sermons is their personal appeal. Morrison spoke directly to the needs and concerns of real people: the grieving, the lonely, the guilt-ridden, the worried, and the spiritually hungry. He described his approach thus, "It has been my habit . . . at the evening service to allow myself a wider scope . . . to win the attention, in honorable ways, of some at least of that vast class of people who today sit so lightly to the church." Judging from the full pews at the Wellington United Free Church, the success of his sermons can be measured by the phrase used in Mark 12:37—"The common people heard him gladly."

In this new edition of Morrison's sermons, Kregel Publications has attempted to "open a window" into the culture of Morrison's ministry and times. Uncommon terms (in today's usage) have been noted, and the frequent quotes, allusions, and personalities identified. In a few places grammatical constructions that might have rolled off the Scottish tongue have been modified with the modern reader in mind. It is our hope that by appreciating the richness of Morrison's style, readers will be encouraged to creatively speak to both the intellect and emotion of today's congregations. Lewis's comments are a fitting encouragement: "Every age has its own outlook. It is especially good at seeing certain truths and specially liable to make certain mistakes. We all, therefore, need the books that will correct the characteristic mistakes of our own period. And that means old books."[3]

DENNIS R. HILLMAN, Senior Editor

---

3. Lewis, 202.

Introduction

Dr. George Herbert Morrison had a gift of saying things that we all would have said, had it occurred to us to say them; and he said those inevitable things as we could not, in English prose that had the effect of "poetry on the heart." This quotation of James Denney aptly sums up the "secret"—if there was such a thing—of Dr. Morrison's classic sermons delivered from his pulpit in Wellington Church, Glasgow, Scotland, from 1902 to 1928.

Throughout his ministry he was known for his concentrated study, his regular pastoral visitation, and his constant writing for publication. His appeal lay not in any physical stature, for he lacked that; not in any tricks or oratory, for he never preached for effect; but in the quiet winsome way in which he spoke to the heart from a heart suffused with the love and grace of Christ. He never lost sight of the fact that as a minister of Christ his first concern must be how best to bring his hearers closer to the heart of the Lord.

Although written early in this century, his sermons are modern in touch and spirit; the tone and temper are admirably effective for use today. Their simplicity of phrase came out of arduous toil as the writer worked in his preparation. The style is the man—quiet and genial—and his preaching was like this. Morrison was always the pastor-preacher, ever seeking to meet life's needs with some word from God.

11

Whatever he did had the hallmark of preparation and finality. Some sermons came easily like the bird on the wing; others came after much hard work and sweat of mind and heart. The fact that he brooded over his texts with something of an artist's unconsciousness and superb leisure is one of the elements in his power as a preacher. He brooded over the Word of God until it became translucent. His loyalty to Christ and his devotion in the secret place are wedded to his daily practice of study and writing.

His counsel to the young preacher is most revealing as the secret of his own success: "I can think of nothing, except that young preachers will do well to guard against the tendency to rush which is the bane of modern life. The habit of unprofitable bustle and rush, the present-day preoccupation with small affairs and engagements, is withholding many good things from us. For myself it is essential that I have leisure to brood and meditate."

To read and study these selections from the author's many volumes of messages will be to open new vistas of truth and to learn how old and familiar truths can be clothed in fresh and living words which will glow with unsuspected meaning.

RALPH G. TURNBULL

Biographical Sketch

I t used to be said that just as visitors to London in bygone days felt that they must of necessity hear Spurgeon or Parker or Liddon, so visitors to Glasgow in more recent years had the feeling that they could not miss hearing Dr. George H. Morrison in Wellington Church. One of the most noted of English Bishops, after fulfilling an afternoon engagement at the University, hurried off to be in time for the evening service at Wellington. And the miner from Fifeshire or the crofter[1] from the Hebrides, spending a Sunday in Glasgow, would have considered the day incomplete if he did not hear Dr. Morrison.

To Glasgow Dr. Morrison's ministry at Wellington was something like what Dr. Alexander Whyte's ministry at St. George's was to Edinburgh. Different in many ways, they were alike in the extent to which they captured the community and maintained their unbroken hold year after year.

Dr. Morrison was a great preacher who was also a great pastor. Of this rather unusual combination he was, indeed, the supreme example.

His genius as a preacher was never more clearly shown than by his success in solving the problem of the second service. Shortly

---

1. a tenant farmer

after his settlement in Glasgow, the afternoon service was giving place to an evening one, but the results in general were not too satisfactory. When Wellington decided on an evening service, Dr. Morrison was determined to give it a distinctive character. In the mornings he adhered to the old Scottish tradition of expository preaching.

In the evenings he allowed himself a wider scope, presenting the Christian essentials in a somewhat different setting and, as he said, calling to his help every type of illustrative aid that appealed to him. He strove to give these evening addresses a strong human interest in order, as he put it, "to win the attention, in honorable ways, of some at least of the vast class of people who sit very lightly to the Church. The touch is naturally far lighter than in the morning, but this does not mean lack of preparation. I prepare as carefully for the one as for the other." His one aim in preaching, he once said, was "to help people along the road." Here I may interpolate how Dr. Morrison once told me that, after he had fully prepared his subject, he set himself the task of striving to see how simply he could present it. His simplicity, therefore, was not the easy, facile thing some may have supposed it to be; it was the fruit of definite and earnest effort.

The response at his evening service was immediate and striking. The church became crowded to overflowing; long queues formed in University Avenue before the doors were opened, and this was no mere passing phase. The same state of matters continued for over twenty-six years, right to the end of his ministry. And he got the class of people he set out to reach. These crowded evening congregations at Wellington made an interesting study in themselves. All classes and all ages were represented, but young men and women were always largely in evidence. Nor were they there because of the prospect of any novelty or sensation. They could only have been drawn because they felt that their wistful longings and inarticulate yearnings were somehow met and answered by the man in the pulpit with the soft voice, the quiet effortless style, and the subtle elusive charm.

There was no clangorous or challenging presentation of a new Evangel. Dr. Morrison's secret was in taking old familiar truths and clothing them in fresh robes of language which made them sparkle with a luster of their own and revealed meanings hitherto hidden and unsuspected. He had a perfect flair in the selection of texts often fresh and suggestive. "He gave them drink out of the depths,"

"In the day that thou stoodest on the other side," "The deep that croucheth beneath," "Thou didst cleave the earth with rivers," are some that may be quoted, almost at random.

Many of his sermons were prose poems; all of them were suffused with a tender charm and rich in spiritual helpfulness. Volume after volume was published, and G. H. Morrison's sermons found a place in manse libraries everywhere, almost like those of F. W. Robertson of Brighton, while they also very markedly appealed to a wide circle of lay readers. They revealed him to be both a mystic and a man of letters and were acknowledged to place him in the foremost ranks of British preachers. . . .

There are many people who still remember this or that sermon of Dr. Morrison's; there are as many who love to recall instances of his pastoral devotion. His routine visitation, so extensive and incessant, was but one feature of his pastoral activity. Many tales could be told of his constant solicitous care of the sick and those in sorrow or trouble. And no success or joy that came to any member of any family in his congregation was overlooked or allowed to pass without letters or postcards from him which are still prized possessions.

The end of this notable ministry came swiftly and unexpectedly when Dr. Morrison was at the age of sixty-two, and while there was no sign of any waning of his powers and no abatement of his popularity. In the first week of October, 1928, he was back from his summer holiday—he held that a good holiday was a *sine qua non*[2] for a minister—and he was getting into the full stream of another winter's activities. On the Wednesday afternoon he had spent three continuous hours in the homes of his people, and in the evening he gave a memorable address to a small company of workers in the hall of Gorbals Church. On Thursday evening he became seriously ill, and on Sunday morning shortly after midnight he passed away almost before his illness had become generally known.

On the day before he died, when there was a slight rally, he was able to have in his hands one of the early copies of a book to which he had been looking forward—his biography, which I had written at the request of London publishers, and in the preparation of which he had given me every facility with his characteristic kindness.

Although Dr. Morrison did not reach the allotted span, he, if any man, had done what he used to call "a good day's darg."[3] He warned

---

2. something essential
3. a good day's work

young preachers against unprofitable bustle and rush and preoccupation with small affairs and trifling engagements. A master of method, he so ordered his time that, while he was never idle, he was never hurried or flurried. There was always about him a calm serenity, and as he moved among men he seemed a living epistle of what he preached. (Reprinted from Alexander Gammie, *Preachers I Have Heard*, Pickering & Inglis, Ltd., London, n.d.)

To heal the broken unity of Christendom,
the scholar may rely on the ultimate
establishment of his critical results; the
ecclesiast may plan treaties of peace and
fusions of doctrine between Church and
Church: but, meanwhile, those who find it
more congenial to pass behind the whole
field of theological divergency, and linger
near the common springs of all human
piety and hope, may perhaps be preparing
some first lines of a true *Eirenikon*.
—James Martineau.

Foreword

These brief addresses, like those of the former volumes of this series, have been prepared from week to week after the more severe preparations for the forenoon diet of worship were completed. It has been my habit at the morning service to handle the greater themes of the Christian revelation and then at the evening worship to allow myself a wider scope, putting essential things in a somewhat different setting and calling to my help every interest I could command. My great aim in this has been to win the attention, in honorable ways, of some at least of that vast class of people who today sit so lightly to the Church. I trust I have not altogether failed in this endeavor; and I gratefully acknowledge a pretty steady inflow of these quiet acknowledgments which art among the most precious seals of ministry

Wellington Church,   George Morrison
Glasgow

Every man at the beginning doth set forth
good wine; and when men have well
drunk, then that which is worse: but thou
has kept the good wine until now
(John 2:10).

1

The Best Wine Last

Into the story of this memorable marriage I do not propose to go
this evening; I wish to base what I may have to say on this remark
of the ruler of the feast. Why, think you, did this saying so impress
John that it lingered ineffaceably in his memory? Was it merely
because of the pleasure it evoked to hear his Master's handiwork so
praised? I think there was a deeper reason. John was by nature an
idealist, loving to find the abstract in the concrete. In the particular
instance of the moment, he was quick to see the universal law. And
it flashed on John, hearing this chairman speak, that he was speaking more wisely than he knew and uttering a truth that had far wider
range than the miracle at that Highland wedding. Was it not true of
many an earthly pageant that the best wine was given at the beginning? Was it not true wherever Christ was active that the best wine
was kept until the end? In other words, take man apart from God
and always it is the worse which follows; but take God in any of
His thousand energies, and always the best is kept until the end.

It is on these two truths I wish to speak tonight, and first on the sadder and more somber of them. Think, then, for a moment of life itself, unsustained by the hope we have in God. Now I am not a pessimist, as you all know; nor am I given to painting dark or lurid pictures; yet the fact is too plain to be gainsaid[1]—afterward that which is worse. First comes childhood with its joy and wonder and with its world compact of mystery and charm. Then follows youth with its ideal and vision and opening manhood with its glowing hopes. And the world is still a very noble place, and the gates of the prison-house have not yet closed, and the body, whether for toil or joy, is still a subtle and a powerful instrument. Then come the heat and battle of mid-life, and the weakness and the weariness of age, and the years when men say, "I have no pleasure in them," and when all the daughters of music are brought low; and the grasshopper shall be a burden, and desire shall fail, and they who were strong men once, shall bow themselves. Is this the gallant youth of long ago, this bent and tottering and palsied form? Are these the eyes that once were bright with love? Is that the brain that was so clear and keen?

> Last scene of all,
> That ends this strange eventful history,
> Is second childishness and mere oblivion,
> Sans teeth, sans eyes, sans taste, sans everything.[2]

Or think again of life's relationships on which the blessing of God is never sought. When character is unchastened and unpurified, how often do the years bring disappointment! Think of the tie of fatherhood and sonship. To the little child the father is a hero. No pictured saint wears such a golden halo as does the father in his children's eyes. His character is flawless and complete—above all question and all criticism; it is the image in the childish mirror of the dim and shadowy character of God. Happy the child who, when its eyes are opened, still finds a character that it can reverence! But if the father is living without God, who swifter to see it than the growing boy? And all that revelation of unworthiness, with occasional glimpses of what is darker still, makes the cup bitter which was once so sweet. And then the words were spoken at a marriage. Are they never true of that most sacred tie? Are there no wives or husbands here tonight who are whispering—afterward that which is

1. denied
2. From *As You Like It* by William Shakespeare (1564–1616).

worse? They remember a day when life was full of courtesy, and of little attentions that were better than gold, and of a charity that suffered long, and of a kindness that was the breath of heaven. Where has it fled to, that kindness of the morning? Who set by the hearth these irritable tempers? Is that cold voice the voice that was so tender in the gentle and sweet days of long ago? Unguarded by the consciousness of God, unchastened by the discipline of watchfulness, unwatered by the kindly dew of prayer, unhelped by the strength made perfect in our weakness, how many homes there are that know too well—afterward that which is worse.

Once more you will think how true this is of sin. It is indeed the masterpiece of evil. It is the token and the triumph of all sin that it always gives the best wine at the start. That is why men of open and generous natures are often those most bitterly assailed. They do not calculate nor look ahead nor reckon seriously with the morrow. And sin is so fair and pleasant at the outset and hides its *afterward* with such consummate mastery, that the reckless heart becomes an easy prey. Do you not think, now, if all the miseries of drunkenness were to meet a man upon the verge of drinking—do you not think he would cry out for help and turn from his accursed vice and flee? But drunkenness does not begin like that. It begins in the social hour and happy comradeship; and only afterward there are the blighted prospects and the shattered body and the ruined home. Let any young man see what I as a minister have seen of the worse-than-death that follows social sin, and he will go home tonight to pray to God for strength to keep himself unspotted from the world. But sin is cunning and conceals all that; it sets on the table a delicious vintage and only afterward—but *always* afterward—that which is worse.

And I cannot leave this darker side of things without asking, must all that stop at death? I wish most passionately I could believe it did; but I see no reasonable ground for that assurance. You tell me that you don't believe in hell. Probably, as you picture it, no more do I. But I believe in law; I believe in immortality; I believe in the momentum of a life. And if the momentum of a life be downward and be unchecked by the strong arm of God, how can we hope that it will be arrested by the frail and yielding barrier of the grave? I hesitate to dwell upon that thought. All I wish to say to you is this. If sin conceals the worse behind tomorrow, may it not conceal the worst behind the grave? Sum up the issues of sin that you have known, the bitterness, the tears, the vain regret; think of its dark-

ened homes, its blighted lives, its wreckage everywhere of broken
hearts; then go, and as you gaze into a lost eternity, say, "Afterward, that which is worse."

But now I turn, and I do so very gladly, to the energies and
activities of God. Wherever God in Christ is working, the best wine
is kept until the end.

Think first for a moment of creation. There was a time, not so
long ago, when religion trembled at the assault of science. It seemed
as if science, flushed with her many victories and pressing forward
to universal conquest, were to drive from the field, in ignominious
rout, many of the truths of revelation. One hears a great deal less of
that today. The combatants have been laying down their arms. They
have been learning that the field of battle was divinely meant to be a
field of brotherhood. And nowhere have they better learned that
lesson than in regard to the method of creation, for scripture and
science are agreed in this, that the best wine was kept until the end.
First there was chaos and the formless deep, then light and the
ingathering of the waters, then the first dawn of life in lowliest
form, mounting into the power of bird and beast. And always, under
the working of that wisdom to which a thousand years are as a day,
the path was upward from dull and shapeless horror to what was
better, richer, and more beautiful. And then at last, not at the first,
came man, capable of communion with his Maker, greater, by that
spark of God within him, than sun and moon and all the host of
heaven. And it is in man, so noble though so fallen, so touched with
heaven although so soiled with hell, that we discover it is the way
of God to keep the best wine until the end.

The same is true in the sphere of revelation, the revelation of the
divine to man. Not all at once, in sudden burst of glory, did God
reveal Himself to human hearts. We speak of revelation as progres-
sive. That is a truth which we insist on now. Only as men are able
to receive it will God reveal the riches of His grace. And so from
age to age men were led on, from the first flush and crimson of the
dawn to the perfect radiance of Him who said, "I am the Light of
the world." Have you ever wondered why God delayed His coming,
why the wheels of His chariot tarried for so long? Compared with
all the ages of mankind, it is but a little while since Christ was here.
But this is the meaning of that long delay, that the God of creation
and of grace is one and that in both activities alike, He keeps the
best wine until the last. You remember how the writer to the He-
brews puts it, in that chapter which we read tonight. "God who at

sundry times and in divers manners spoke in time past unto the fathers by the prophets, hath in these last days spoken unto us by His Son." Precious are the promises of the Old Testament. Precious are the teachings of the prophets. Precious is every gleam that was vouchsafed[3] to the waiting heart of patriarch and psalmist. But it is when we turn to Christ, the Son of God, the Way, the Truth, the Life, the Resurrection, that we cry with the ruler of the feast at Cana, "Thou hast kept the best wine until now."

I think, too, we may apply this thought to the life of the incarnate Lord Himself. It was all blessed, yet it was *most* blessed, not in its beginning but its end. I turn to the manger-cradle by the inn, when I wish to fathom His humiliation. I turn to His words and to His perfect life, when I wish to know the fatherhood of God. But when I realize I am a sinner and that my deepest need is pardon and release, then it is "Rock of ages cleft for me, let me hide myself in Thee." Not on the teaching of Christ is the church built, although that teaching shall never pass away. Not on the example of Christ is the church built, though that example be its spur and goal. The church of God is built upon redemption, on pardon and peace that have been won through death; and that is why Christendom has looked to Calvary and said, "Thou hast kept the best wine until now." If the Sermon on the Mount were the whole gospel, I confess that I could hardly understand it. It is so unlike all that we know of God to give all that is best at the beginning. But if the Sermon on the Mount be but a step in the ladder that leads upward to the Cross, then, in the life and death of Jesus, I am in touch with the ways of the divine. It is that fact—the fact of a redemption—that fills and floods the apostolic page. It is that fact that has made the cross the universal symbol of the gospel. "This cup is the New Testament in My blood, shed for many for the remission of sins." Ah yes, thou hast kept the best wine until now.

Lastly, and in a word or two, is not this true also of our Christian calling? The path of the just is as the shining light which shines more and more unto the perfect day. Not all at once does Christ reveal Himself, when we go forward determined to be His. And the old life still struggles for the mastery, and we are in heaviness through manifold temptations. But the difference between Christ and the devil is just this, that the devil's tomorrow is worse than his today; but the morrow of Christ, for every man who trusts Him, is

---

3. granted

always brighter and better than His yesterday. Every act of obedience that we do gives us a new vision of His love. Sorrow and trial reveal His might of sympathy, as the darkness of the night reveals the stars. And when at last the wrestling is over, and like tired children we lie down to sleep, and when we waken and behold His face in the land where there is no more weariness, I think we shall look back upon it all and find new meanings in every hour of it; but I think also we shall cry adoringly, "Thou hast kept the best wine until now."

Jesus saith unto him, I am the way, the
truth, and the life; no man cometh unto the
Father by Me (John 14:6).

2

Christ and the Intellect

One of the features of the present day is the emphasis which is
laid upon intelligence. There is an intellectual culture now accessi-
ble to many that once was the possession of the few. Great men are
singularly rare just now, but clever men are singularly plentiful—
indeed, by the use of that word "clever" alone, one might conjecture
the prevailing temper. For few words are more often on men's lips,
none are more liberally used in praise, and a hundred failings are
forgiven a man who has the reputation of being clever. It would be
interesting to investigate the causes that have led to this strong
accent on intelligence. Partly it is the inevitable outcome of the
intellectual triumphs of past years. And partly it springs from fiercer
competition, where dullness finds itself increasingly discounted, and
where one of the first conditions of success is an alert and capable
intelligence.

In view, then, of that feature of our time, there is one question of
very vital interest. That is, what is Christ's doctrine of the intellect—what are our Savior's ethics of the mind? We know how
Christ has affected our emotional life, expanding our sympathies
into undreamed-of fullness. We know how He has changed the life

25

of action, investing the lowliest drudgery with splendor. But what I want to try to find tonight is not Christ's attitude to work or feeling. It is the attitude of Christ to thought—the way in which He viewed the intellect.

Now at first glance it might be said—and has been said—that Christ disparaged the intellectual life. Think, for example, of the great simplicity that marks His teaching in the first three gospels. Other teachers are hard to understand; they make instant and large demands upon the intellect. Christ casts His message into a form so simple that it would not stumble the intelligence of a child. The teaching that is congenial to the intellect is teaching that is shaped into a system. Christ had no system—no elaboration—He was spontaneous and perfectly occasional. The teaching that is to win the intellect must clothe itself in the language of the intellect. But the language of Christ is vividly pictorial; it is the speech of the imagination and the heart. All these are facts that he who runs may read. They are characteristics of the Savior's method. And men—not irreverent men—have taken them to indicate a certain disparagement of intellect.

Or think of the friends and companions of the Lord—the kind of people He loved to have around Him. You would never dream of calling them clever people. They were in no sense intellectual persons. As a matter of fact, the intellectuals of that day were the persons who are known as Sadducees. It was they who had thought most deeply on great questions. It was they who had the courage of their convictions. And yet the relations of Jesus with the Sadducees were very seldom those of comradeship; they were almost always those of stern antagonism. No one pictures the sweet home at Bethany as a home distinguished for its mental culture. There is not a sign that the disciples, before Calvary, were men of high or exceptional intelligence. And the very fact that Jesus chose such friends and liked to talk with them and loved to dwell with them has been regarded on the part of Christ as implying a certain disparagement of intellect.

But such a view is effectually dispelled when we begin to look a little closer. There may have been things which Jesus Christ belittled, but the intelligence of man was not among them. He did not deify it, and He did not isolate it. He never dreamed it could answer every question. But He recognized to the full its place and power and breathed on it a new and ampler life.

Think, for example, of that scene in the Temple when He went up to Jerusalem, a boy of twelve. "Wist ye not that I must be about My Father's business?" It was one of the great hours in Christ's career. It was an hour of spiritual awaking, when the purpose of His life began to glow before Him. Now rose, in quivering outline on His soul, the vision of what He was destined to fulfill. Yet it is notable that in that spiritual crisis the intellect of Jesus was not slumbering but was kindled to a pitch of high activity and moved in the sweet freedom of delight. He was only a boy among the temple doctors, yet with what intense ardor did He question them. And His words were so searching and so true when He replied that we read they were astonished at His answers. Here was not only a mighty soul on fire—here was a mighty intellect on fire, and both were burning into a single flame. There are men who only gain their spiritual raptures by lulling their intelligence asleep. It was never so in the life of Jesus Christ. It should never be so with any of His followers. God was most real to Christ and heaven most near, not when He gave an opiate to His mind, but when that mighty and unmatched intelligence was working at its clearest and its best.

Then again, you can often discover a man's attitude by the kind of word that is frequent on his lips. Unless a man is a consummate hypocrite, out of the fullness of the heart the mouth will speak. "Thy speech betrayeth thee" was true of Simon; but it is true of millions besides Simon. Every man has his familiar words, and such are as a lattice to his soul. Now when we read the Gospel of St. John, we light on one of these words of Jesus Christ. He used it constantly. He loved to linger on it. It was full of hidden music for the Master. Can you think of the favorite word that I refer to? It was the great word *truth*. Not love, that is a word of tenderest feeling; not power, that is redolent of will. Had love and power been the only great words of Christ, one might have held that He disparaged intellect. But when in the richest and the deepest gospel you hear the Savior saying, "I am the *truth*," you hear Him claiming to be the Lord of intellect, the Redeemer of the soul.

Now the way in which Jesus used that word gives us an insight into His view of intellect. Christ will have nothing of the culture of the brain at the expense of the culture of the character. The great word of Plato is the word *idea*, and an idea is purely intellectual. One of the leading words of Solomon is knowledge, and knowledge must ever reside within the mind. But Christ never breathes a whisper of "idea," nor does He linger tenderly on "knowledge." His word is truth; and truth, born in the intellect, takes the whole character within its grip. "Sanctify them through Thy truth, Thy word is truth"—then truth has got a sanctifying power. "The truth shall make you free"—then truth is mighty not only over prejudice but over passion. "I am the truth"—then truth is broad as man and high and deep as human personality. In other words, the Christian intellect must work in harmony with the whole Christian character. A purely intellectual person may be clever, but most assuredly he is not Christian. The mark of a Christian is not mental brilliance; it is an intellect which so ennobles character that heart and will and passion and intelligence unite together to the praise of God.

This leads me to say a word in passing about the greatest intellectual sin in Christ's eyes. What feature, think you, of the mental life was darkest and most guilty to our Lord? Was it ignorance? Think of Him on the cross, crying "Father, forgive them, they know not what they do." Was it doubt? Think of Him with Thomas, "Thomas, reach hither thy hand and feel the wound-print!" Christ was not harsh and terrible with doubters. Christ had an infinite pity for the ignorant. It was not to be ignorant that damned a man. What damned him was to be unteachable. "Except ye become as little children, ye cannot even see the kingdom of God." The one condition of entrance to the best was to be childlike, teachable, receptive. And so conversely to be fixed and final—to have every window closed and gateway barred—was the one way to lose the breath of heaven and to miss the gentle footfall of the angels. It is not doubt that is faith's opposite. Doubt sometimes is but faith disguised. The opposite of faith is that finality which does not believe in larger truth tomorrow. Faith throws the lattice back—unbars the door—waits for new messengers across the hills. Faith is expectant, eager, childlike, buoyant. Its opposite is not doubt, but death.

It is notable also in Christ's doctrine of the intellect what a great stress He put upon obedience. "If any man willeth to do His will, He shall know of the doctrine whether it be of God." It is not merely by learning that we know. It is by all that we are—all that we strive to be. There is not a worthy deed we ever do but brightens and deepens our intellectual life. I have known more than one Highland saint who never had any intellectual training. They had had little schooling, they never were at college, and their libraries were of the scantiest kind. Yet in every true sense of the word they were men of culture; their language was choice and their thoughts large and just; and they had singular power in complicated questions of seizing on the things that really mattered. What was the secret of that mental clarity?—"If any man willeth to do His will." To God they had prayed—in Christ's name they had wrestled—they had clung to the right and beaten down the wrong; until at last that life of deep obedience—that faithfulness to God in what was least—all unexpectedly had reached their intellect and made it a sphere of mastery and joy. You will never think rightly if you are living wrongly. Impure passions mean an untrue intellect. Let a man deliberately ignore his plainest duty, and there is not a thought he thinks but will be tainted by it. But on the other hand let a man take up his burden and do now what he knows he ought to do, and that will do more to brighten his intelligence than the dull reading of a score of books. "I am the *truth*," says Jesus Christ to us; but remember He says first, "I am the *way*." That is the order which Jesus Christ insists on—first doing, at the bidding of conscience and of God, then knowing. If any man wills to do God's will—says God helping me I shall be true to what is best— he shall know; it will illuminate his intellect and be a secret of truest culture.

And do you see why Christ insists on this? It is because of His great love for poor and lowly people. He wants them to know that however hard their lot, the truest culture is at their command. Tell the world that intellectual excellence is only to be attained by toil-some study, and immediately to a hundred thousand toilers you make the intellectual life impossible. But tell the world that perception springs from character, that nothing so purifies the eye as duty done, and to the weariest toiler in the shop or home you open the gates of intellectual progress. Christ has no quarrel with the earnest student. His blessing and benediction are upon him. But He sees the multitude who cannot study, who are leisureless and bent in the grim battle; and it is to them, just where their lot is cast and under the very burdens they must bear, that Jesus by His doctrine of obedience makes a way to the intellectual life. You cannot be learned? At least you can be pure. You are dull? Heroes are often dull. You have no leisure day by day to study? But you *have* leisure to abhor that which is evil. And if you do it and cleave to what is good and play the man and take up your cross bravely, the intellectual wilder-ness of yesterday will begin to rejoice and blossom as the rose. Better is the little that the good man knows than the encyclopedic learning of the bad. When a man is out of living touch with God, he can see nothing in its true relationship. And culture is not knowing many things, it is rather seeing what we know in true relationships, reaching its highest when everything we know is "bound by gold chains about the feet of God."[1]

In closing, let me say one other word. It is on the influence of immortality on intellect. Jesus has quickened and steadied human intellect by bringing immortality to light. "Now we know in part," says the apostle, and the wisest can but bow the head to that. We cannot grasp the least in its entirety, nor can we complete the mystic circle here. And if death ends all, then *all* is never known; the truth full-orbed is never to be ours; the cup is held by a retreating angel, to be dashed into a thousand fragments at the grave. But Christ hath brought immortality to light. "Then shall we know, even as we are known." High above intellect shines like a star of hope the vision of perfect and eternal life. And if the intellect of Christendom has faced its tasks with an undaunted and unwavering fortitude, it owes not a little of that high persistence to the revelation of immortality in Christ.

---

1. From "In Memoriam" by Alfred (Lord) Tennyson (1809–1894), English poet.

He giveth His beloved [in] sleep
(Ps. 127:2).

3

The Gifts of Sleep

If we take the words of our text just as they stand, they are charged with deep and beautiful significance. They tell us what our own experience confirms, that sleep is the gift of God. The world has gifts which it gives to its favorite children. It loads them with wealth or with honor or with fame. But God deals otherwise with His beloved, for "He giveth to His beloved sleep." It would, of course, be very wrong to say that sleeplessness is a mark of the divine displeasure. A man may be wrapped in the gracious peace of God yet seek in vain the quieting of slumber. Yet is it true that sleep, when it is given, is such a medicine for weariness and travail that it can be nothing save the gift of love. I think of Jesus in the storm-tossed boat, asleep on the pillow when all were in wild alarm. I think of Peter fast asleep in prison, when the morrow was to see his execution. I think of the tired worker when comes nightfall and of the sufferer who has been racked through weary hours, and I learn how tenderly and deeply true is this: He giveth His beloved sleep. Nor can one ever ignore that sweetest of all suggestions wherein the word is whispered over the sleep of death. A thousand memories of shadow and of tears have flustered around that inter-pretation. It is when after life's fever one sleeps well, when the

31

struggle has ended and quiet peace has fallen; it is then that love, through the mist of weeping, murmurs: "so He *giveth* His beloved sleep."

But though that is a comforting and blessed truth, it is not the true interpretation of the words. If you read the verse in relation to the context, you will see that that could hardly be the meaning. The psalmist is warning against that overwork which so surely degenerates into worry. He is picturing the man who overdrives himself until he has no leisure and no liberty. And all this pressure and feverish activity is not only in the sight of God a sin, it is also, says the psalmist, a mistake. It is vain for you to rise up early and to sit up late. You will never gain the choicest things that way. Let a man be feverish, overstrained, unrested, and he is sure to miss the worthiest and the best. God giveth to His beloved *in* sleep—when they are at rest like a child within its cradle, when they are freed from that turbulence of wild desire wherein the still small voice is quite inaudible. Remember that the psalmist never dreamed of casting a slur on honest, manly labor. He knew too well the blessings that we win and the sins that we are saved from by our work. What was borne in upon his soul was this, that by overtoil we lose more than we gain, for many of the richest gifts of heaven only approach us as by the path of slumber. It is imperative that the soul should be held passive, if we are to have the inflow of His grace. It is imperative that its uproar should be hushed, if we are to catch the music of the faraway. And it is that which the psalmist hints at here, when, in the intense language of a poet, he cries to men, "Your stress and strain are vanity; God giveth to His beloved in sleep."

Now let me set that thought in one or two relationships, thinking first of the blessings of our infancy. There is a world of love encompassing an infant, yet how unconscious the babe is of it all! When our Savior was drawing near the cross, He said to His disciples, "I go to prepare a place for you," and they knew from that hour that when they woke in glory they would find that all was ready for their coming. But not alone in the land beyond the river is a place prepared for every one God loves. When into this present life a child awakes, hearts have been busy with the preparation. Stooping over it there is a mother's love and all the splendor of a mother's patience. Shielding it there is a father's strength, and to provide for all its needs, a father's labor. And it is clad and fed with food convenient, and cradled to rest and sheltered from the storm. And should it ail, the best skill in the city is urgently summoned to the tiny sufferer. What a wealth of love and of love's care is here, yet who more passive than that little infant! Have these small hands helped in the preparation? Has that new heart done any of the planning? Helpless it lies, and doomed to certain death, if life depended on its puny efforts. But "God giveth to His beloved in sleep."

Again our text has a great depth of meaning when we think of the influences that play upon our youth. We shall never have worthy views of education if we forget the truth which it conveys. I suppose there was never a time in the world's history when education was so organized as it is now. The day has long since passed into oblivion when any man would do to be a schoolmaster. And instead of these dark and dirty little places which were once dignified with the high name academy, we have the spacious and often stately buildings which are so conspicuous in every city. All this is eloquent of educating zeal, but I shall tell you something that is still more eloquent. It is to find the schoolroom on some lonely island around which swirls and sweeps a dangerous tide. It is to go to the remotest glen, which often in winter-storm is inaccessible, and light there upon the modest schoolhouse and the children gathered in it round their teacher.

Now, brethren, all this is excellent, and for it all we thank God and take courage. But never let us forget that, after all, this is but a part of education. Great is the influence of every schoolroom in quickening the brain and molding character; but mightier influences than any teacher wields are being wielded beyond the classroom walls; and all the time, in play-hour and in holiday and in the loving relationship of home, there is progressing a deeper education than has ever been dreamed of in the standards. Its lesson book is not the printed page; it is the happy companionship of boyhood. Its map is not the chart upon the wall; it is the burn and the hillside where the heather grows. By friendship with its quarrel and temptation, by the daily pressure of a mother's goodness, by the scene that meets the eye before the cottage, by golden mornings and still and starry nights, by all this and by much more than this is education ceaselessly advancing. It is these memories which will return amid the jar and uproar of the city. It is these which will be a haven of sweet rest when the land of youth is many a league away. Yet how absolutely and utterly unconscious is the youth in the glad morning of his days of the blessings which are ingathering on him so and which are to make him rich through all the years. For him the burn is but the place to fish in, and sunset but a bitter call to bed, and friends are but a necessity for play, and home is but a necessity for food. Asleep to all that his youth is going to mean for him, he passes through his glad and golden years; but "God giveth to His beloved in sleep."

This thought, too, helps to explain the silence that surrounds the boyhood of our Lord. It is akin to the silence we observe when someone is sleeping in the chamber near us. It is true that Christ, far earlier than most, awoke to the majesty of His vocation. He was only a boy of twelve when in the Temple He said, "Wist ye not that I must be about My Father's business?" Yet the very fact that this story is enshrined so declares that this was a memorable moment when much that had been slumbering before leaped up in an intense realization. It was not in the village school that Christ received the lessons which were to bless humanity. It was as He played in the meadows and moved among the hills and opened His heart to the living joy of nature. It was as He dwelt in His quiet and happy home, where the father feared God and did his duty and where the mother's presence was a benediction in its watchful and meditative love. All this, just because He was a child, Jesus would unconsciously receive. All this, because He was a sinless child, He would receive intensely and indelibly. And hence the silence of the gospel narrative that will not force itself with noisy footstep into the place where God with liberal hand is giving to His beloved as in sleep.

Once again our text has large significance in regard to the pursuit of happiness. If anywhere in life, it is just there that it is vain to rise up early and to sit up late. Not when we are determined, come what may, to have a pleasant and a happy life; not then, as the reward of that insistence, does God bestow the music of the heart. He gives it when there is forgetfulness of self and the struggle to be true to what is highest, though the morning break without a glimpse of blue and the path be through the valley of the shadow. The one sure way to miss the gift of happiness is to rise early and to sit up late for it. To be bent at every cost on a good time is the sure harbinger of dreary days. It is when we have the courage to forget all that and to lift up our hearts to do the will of God, that, like a swallow flashing from the eaves, happiness glances out with glad surprise. Had Jesus lived just that He might be happy, He certainly would have escaped the cross. None would have laughed Him to scorn in Jairus' house; none would have pierced Him in His hands and feet. But He came not to be ministered unto but to minister and to give His life a ransom for many; and so you have Him talking of His joy. Brethren, especially those of you who are still young, remember that God means you to be happy. Nine-tenths of our unhappiness is selfishness and is an insult cast in the face of God. But the way to be happy is not to toil for happiness. It is to be awake to what is higher. And then, as the day goes on, comes the discovery that God gives to His beloved in sleep.

Lastly, and in a word or two, that I may not close without remembering those who mourn, I want you to think how true this is of heaven. The last best gift of a kind God is heaven, and God gives it to His beloved in sleep. How it would have been had man not sinned and fallen, there is little need that we inquire. Like Enoch, man would have walked with God, until his never-halting footsteps had won home. But death has passed upon all men for that all have sinned; yet, "O death, where is thy victory?" God makes thy foul embrace His opportunity; He gives to His beloved while they sleep. As one stands with sorrowing heart beside the dead and looks on lips from which the breath has flown, it is very strengthening and very soothing to say, "God gives sleep to His beloved." But is it not better to lift the eyes to heaven and, thinking of its liberty and joy, to say, as the brow is kissed for the last time, "He giveth to His beloved in sleep."

He rebuked the winds and the sea, and
there was a great calm (Matt. 8:26).

4

The Restfulness of Christ

There are some people whom we meet with as we journey who
impress us with a sense of restfulness. Such people, not infrequently,
are men; more often, if I mistake not, they are women. They are not
necessarily brilliant, nor have they any striking or unusual gifts; all
we feel is that in their company there is a pleasant atmosphere of
restfulness. We are all tempted to strain after effect sometimes, but
in the presence of these people we do not think of that. There is no
effort to keep up conversation. We are not ashamed even of being
silent. Like a breath of evening after the garish day, when coolness
and quiet have followed on the sunshine, such natures, often we
know not how, enwrap us with a sweet sense of rest

And you will find, as your survey of life broadens, that people
who are weak never create that atmosphere. There may be many
vices in the strong, but there is always something unrestful in the
weakling. We talk of the restfulness of the calm summer evening,
and unhappy is the man who never feels it. But we know now how
at the back of that there is the stress of conflict and the strain of
battle. And so in the people who are full of restfulness, could we but
read the story of their lives, we should find the record of many a
hard battle and the tale of many a well-contested field. I do not

mean that they have done great deeds. I do not mean that they have suffered terribly. The greatest victories are not spectacular nor is there any crowd to cheer the combatant. I only mean that people who are restful are people who have looked facts in the face, who have toiled when there was not much light to toil by and carried their crosses in a smiling way. There is never any rest in weakness. To be weak is miserable, doing or suffering, says Milton.[1] The condition of all restfulness is power of the open-eyed and quiet heroic kind. And probably that is why people who are restful are at the same time delightfully subduing; for there is nothing so subdues a man as power, save the apotheosis[2] of power, which is love.

Now no man can reasonably doubt that Jesus was preeminently restful. Whenever I peruse the gospel story, I am impressed by the restfulness of Christ. One of the first invitations which He gave was this: "Come unto Me and I will give you rest." One of the last promises before the Cross was this: "My peace I give unto you." And though there are depths in the peace of Jesus Christ that reach to the deepest abysses of the soul, yet the words would have been little else than mockery had the Christ not been wonderfully restful. Take a word like that of the Apostle Paul: "The Lord of peace give you peace alway." Down to the depths of the sin-pardoned soul you are still in the province of the benediction. But there never could have been that benediction unless the Lord, whom the church loved and worshiped, had impressed everyone who ever met Him with the feeling of an infinitude of rest.

And I cannot help thinking that if men realized that, it would constitute a new appeal for Christ. If I know anything about this present day, there is a craving in its heart for restfulness. Mr. Moody[3] used to tell a story of a little child who was tossing and fretting in some childish fever. And its mother sang to it and told it stories, and the little child tossed and was fretful still. And then the mother stooped down without a word and gathered her little daughter in her arms, whereon the child, in an infinite content, said, "Ah, Mother, *that's* what I wanted." She did not know what she wanted, like many wiser people; but like most of us, she knew it when she got it. And so today there are a thousand voices singing to us and some perhaps telling stories. But it seems to me that the times are a little

---

1. From "Paradise Lost" by John Milton (1608–1674), English poet.
2. deified or glorified ideal
3. Dwight L. Moody (1837–1899), American evangelist.

fevered, that the pulse is not beating steadily like our fathers', and that what we need in modern society is just the shadow and the space of rest. The strenuous life is being overdone. It is a little too strenuous to be strong. It is issuing not in the dignity of manhood but in the hustle of the modern market. And wise men everywhere are coming to see that we need a new ideal not less intense, but one that has ampler room within its borders for the fructifying pleasantness of rest.

It is just here that, out of the mist of ages, there steps the figure of the Man of Nazareth. "Come unto Me and I will give you rest"—it is the message of Jesus for today. I want you to remember that these words were spoken to men and women whose burden was religion. It was the spirit of the age, charged with tradition, from which our Savior offered them relief. And once again the spirit of the age demands an ideal that shall have room for rest, and standing among us is the restful Christ. Now if Christ had been an idle Oriental, I should never have pled His fitness for today. You will never transplant the dreamy idle East to the practical, vigorous, insistent West. But the continual wonder about Christ is this, that in every part and power of His being He was intensely and unceasingly alive with a vitality which puts us all to shame. Let a woman touch Him in the throng—"Who touched Me?" Let Him see a crowd, and He is "moved with compassion." Let Him be baited by the subtlest doctors, and He fences and parries with superb resource. In body and spirit, in will, emotion, intellect, Christ was so flooded with the tides of life, that when he cried to men, "I am the *Life*," they felt in a moment that the word was true. Yet, "Come unto Me and I will give you rest." That is the abiding mystery of Christliness. That is the secret we are hungering for today, how to engraft the strenuous on the restful. And you may laboriously search the ages and all the ideals and visions of the ages and never find these so perfectly combined as in the historic personality of Jesus. The East says, "Come let us rest awhile; no need to hurry, and the sun is warm." And the West says, "Let us be up and doing," until we have almost lost the forest for the trees. And then comes Jesus, most superbly active and toiling with an inspired assiduity, and yet in the very thick and tangle of it, girt with a restfulness that is divine.

Now when we study the life of Jesus Christ, we light on one or two sources of this restfulness. And in the first place it was the restfulness of balance. You remember how John in the Book of Revelation has a vision of the heavenly Jerusalem; and you remember how, as he surveys its form, he sees that the length and the breadth and the height of it are equal. It was symmetrical in every measurement—perfectly balanced in every dimension, and I challenge any man to read the gospel and not remark that equipoise in Christ. We talked of Bismarck[4] as the man of iron, but we never talk of the iron will of Christ. We speak of the myriad-mindedness of Shakespeare,[5] but we do not speak in that fashion about Jesus. And it is not reverence that keeps us silent nor is it any awe at present deity; it is rather that everything is in such perfect poise there, that the total impression is repose. It is the same in the highest works of art. In the noblest art there is always a great restfulness. Passion is there, and energy, and power, as there are passion and power in the sunrise. But the mark of genius is the mark of God, that it brings the warring forces into balance and holds its energies in such a poise that the impression of the whole is rest. It is not the enthusiast who is most like Christ, no matter how fiery his ardor be. It is not the man whose feelings are the most tender. It is not the man who has a will of steel. Ethically, that man is most like Christ who has so lived with Him under the love of God that every part and power of his being has opened out like a flower to the sun. That, then, is one of the ethical sources of what I call the restfulness of Christ. Ill-balanced men always make us restless; ill-balanced women do so even more. But to me, at least, reading the life of Jesus, there comes such a sense of powers in perfect balance, that I accept with all my heart the invitation, "Come unto Me and I will give you rest."

Again it is the restfulness of purpose—of steady and unalterable purpose. There is no rest in the little Highland burn[6] as it brawls and chafes along its bed of granite. It "chatters, chatters as it goes," and chattering things and people are not restful. But the mighty river, silent and imperial, guiding its wealth of water to the sea, is like a parable of mighty purpose, and in the bosom of that purpose there is rest. There is something river-like about the life of Christ—it is so resistless in its flow. Sorrows or joys could no more stop His course than the lights and shadows on the hills can stop the Clyde.[7] And in this mighty purpose, so deep and so divine, there lies not a little of

4. Otto von Bismarck (1815–1898), German statesman, first chancellor of the German Empire 1871–1890.

5. William Shakespeare (1564–1616, English poet and dramatist.

6. brook

7. river in southern Scotland

the secret of the unfailing restfulness of Christ. Why is it that young men are so restless? And why is there generally more repose as life advances? It is not merely that the fires are cooling; it is that life is settling into a steadier aim. No longer do we beat at doors that will not open—no longer does every by-path suggest dreams—we have found our work and we have strength to do it, and in that concentration there is rest. Now in the life of Jesus Christ there is always the beat of underlying purpose. No life was so free or so happily spontaneous. To call it cribbed, cabined, and confined were mockery. Yet underneath its gladness and its reach and all the splendor and riches of its liberty, there is a burning and dominating purpose, and in the bosom of that purpose is repose. It is a bad thing not to have a friend. It is a worse thing not to have a purpose. Something to love, to fight for, and to live for in the heat of the battle keeps a man at rest. And Jesus had the world to love and fight for and the world's redemption to achieve on Calvary, and I say that *that*, in the midst of all the tumult, was the strain of music whose echo was repose.

Then lastly it was the restfulness of trust. Christ had repose because He trusted so. Faithlessness, even in the relationships of earth, is the lean and hungry mother of unrest. Let a mistress once distrust her maid, and there will be worrying suspicion every day. Let a husband distrust his wife, a wife her husband, and the peace of home, sweet home, is in its ashes. We charge this with being a restless age, and we lay the blame of that restlessness on love of pleasure, but I question if it be not lack of faith that is the true root of social instability. To me the wildest little child is restful, and it is restful because it trusts me so. Faith is the great rebuke of boisterous winds when the ship is like to be swamped in angry waters. And the perfect restfulness of Jesus Christ, in a life of unceasing movement and demand, sprung from a trust in God that never faltered even amid the bruisings of the Cross.

The manna ceased on the morrow after
they had eaten of the old corn of the land
(Josh. 5:12).

5

The Ceasing of the Manna

The giving of the manna to the Israelites was one of the most notable providences of the exodus. It happened when the pilgrims had struck inland and were faced with the starvation of the desert. The desert was probably more fertile then than it is now, but even then it was utterly inadequate to provide for that mighty and marching company. Faced by certain starvation, as they thought, we can hardly wonder that Israel began to murmur. "Would to God," they cried, "we had been left to die in Egypt, where at least we had food to satisfy our hunger." And it was then, in the hour of their extremity when faced by the gaunt specter of starvation, that God wrought the miracle of manna. From that day onward it had never failed, in spite of all murmuring and all rebellion. If the gifts of God depended on man's faith, the manna would have vanished very quickly. But day after day, through fret and sin and cowardice, God held to His purpose, as He always does, for the long-suffering of God is our salvation.[1] But now the forty years' journeying was over. The need was gone, and so the manna ceased. Israel awoke, and the ground was no longer white; it was all golden with the ripened corn.

---

1. See 2 Peter 3:15.

41

And I think you can picture the look of wild astonishment which would flash in an instant into a thousand eyes on that morning of the ceasing of the manna. There was deep doctrine in the giving of the manna. There was doctrine not less deep in its withdrawal. God had His lessons to teach Israel then and through Israel to teach us all. And so tonight, speaking in modern language and thinking of our own needs and lives, I want to touch on the interior meanings that are wrapped up in the ceasing of the manna.

In the first place the ceasing of the manna should teach us that there is inevitable loss in all our gains. It was a great thing for Israel to gain the plains of Jericho, but when they had done so, they lost the bread of angels. For forty years they had been struggling forward to win the land of their hopes and of their dreams. Now it was theirs—they stood upon its soil; all they had battled and toiled for had been crowned. But now that it was theirs, the manna ceased; the miracle of every morning was no more; and dimly this stubborn people would perceive that something is lost with everything we gain.

Now we talk sometimes about the gains of our losses, and it is true that we often gain by what we lose. There are many people who were never rich until God in His providence had made them poor. If we would win ourselves we must first lose ourselves—there is he that scatters and yet increases—that is the first lesson every man must learn who seeks to follow in the steps of Christ. But remember that if we gain by what we lose, it is also true that we lose by what we gain. At every step we take, something must go—something perhaps which we reckoned precious yesterday. And he alone is wise and brave and cheerful who recognizes that inevitable law and presses forward, undaunted, to the best with the courage to forget what is behind. We gain the promised land and lose the manna. We gain experience and lose the morning dew. We gain the strength and energy of manhood and lose the freshness and wonder of the child. We gain the peace and the beauty of old age and lose the strength and energy of manhood. No man will ever succeed in this hard world who has not learned the art of concentration. There is no eminence today for any man who cannot say with the apostle, "This one thing I do." Yet in a world so rich, so full of voices, so teeming and tingling with ten thousand interests, who does not feel that if we gain by concentrating, there is much that we inevitably lose? Is there no gain in suffering when it is sanctified? Have we never known lives which a great sorrow deepened? It would be a shallow, unbrotherly, and heartless world but for the shadow and the furnace and the cross. Yet with all sorrow, though brought to the feet of God and irradiated with the light of immortality, there is something that goes—something that made sweet music—something that never will be ours again. Now these are facts, and a wise man faces facts. He does not murmur nor cry for the impossible. He sets his face steadfastly toward Jerusalem and turns his back upon his boyhood's Galilee. For he knows that though the manna be withdrawn, there will still be the ingathering of the autumn, and he lifts up his eyes, and the fields are white to harvest, "some thirty, some sixty, and some an hundredfold."

Again, the ceasing of the manna teaches us to be very cautious in asserting that anything is indispensable. If there was one thing graven upon the heart of Israel, it was that without the manna they could not live at all. Remember that of those who had left Egypt, only Caleb and Joshua now survived. All the others had been born out in the wilderness and were children of desert air and desert nurture. The first thing that had caught their eye had been the manna. The first food they had tasted had been manna. As children, as boys, as men in the prime of manhood, it was manna that had stood between them and death; until at last, after these years of nurture, of daily and unvarying dependence, there was not a man in Israel but would think that manna was indispensable to him. Then in the plain of Jericho the manna ceased. The morning dawned when the manna was not there. For the first time in nine-and-thirty years the ground was not white with sustenance from heaven. And did they perish then, or did God let them starve? Was there nothing but manna between them and death? They had to learn their lesson from that failure that God fulfills Himself in many ways. The manna ceased, but the harvesting began. The manna ceased, but they still lived and prospered. The manna ceased, but they were strong for battle and more than conquerors though it was gone. And I am sure that as they thought of that—as they sat and talked by the camp fires at night—the church of the Old Testament would learn that all is not indispensable that seems so.

There is no word, I think, more needed today for the church militant of the New Testament. There is no worse service that any man can render than calling that indispensable which is not really so. Some things *are* vital to life and to salvation, and to these we must hold in the teeth of all defiance; but apart from these I beg you to be cautious in saying that this or that is indispensable. We have all been fed on certain views of truth just as the Israelites were fed on manna. We have looked at the Bible in a certain way since we were children at our mother's knee. And so wedded were we to that precious nurture and to the tender memories with which it is inwoven, that to some of us it seemed that we must starve if we were bereft of the manna of our youth. Then came the morning when the manna ceased. Our intellect awoke and it was gone. New truths arrested us—new thoughts of revelation—fresh insight into the ways of God in nature; and the strange thing is that *then* we did not starve but were fed upon the finest of the wheat. Christ became real to us His love became more wonderful; the purposes of God grew more magnificent. The manna of our unthinking childhood ceased only to lead us to the harvest-field. And so we have learned in the conflict of today, when the faith of Jesus is fighting for its life, to be very cautious lest we harm the cause by saying that this or that is indispensable. The one thing vital is that Jesus came and lived and died as a sacrifice and rose. Fix the one point of the compass fast in that, and let the other swing widely as you please. There is much that may seem to you as indispensable as the manna of the desert seemed to Israel, yet the manna ceased and Israel did not starve.

Once more, the ceasing of the manna gave to Israel new views of the presence and providence of God. It taught them to see God in common things and to realize His presence in the fields. The manna was not natural; it was a miracle. It was a striking and supernatural provision. It came from heaven—it was the bread of angels; it was not part of the economy of nature. And so when the children of Israel thought of providence, and when they meditated on the care of God, that care for them would always be associated with wonderful and strange interpositions. But the day came when the manna ceased to fall; the providence of God was shifted elsewhere. It was transferred from the miracle of manna to the corn that ripened in a thousand fields. And you see, do you not, what that achieved for Israel, and how it taught them larger views of providence, for the God of the manna and the God of miracle had become the God who ripens every harvest. No longer in an isolated miracle did Israel find the hand of the divine. The manna ceased—they were cast back on nature to find in nature the same care of God. And so they learned what is so hard to learn, that providence had a wider reach than once they dreamed, and that the common field may be as full of heaven as the manna which is the bread of angels.

Now it is not very hard for any man to feel that God is near in the

great hours. In a great sorrow or an overwhelming loss there is
something that whispers He is not far away. How many a man who
never recks[2] of heaven, has cried out in some great agony, "My
God." How many a man who has not prayed for years, in shipwreck
or accident prays with all his heart. We are touched with the sense
of the infinite in such great hours; we feel our utter need of the
divine. But the question I want to ask of you tonight is how is it
with you when the manna ceases? When there is nothing startling
or arresting, what do you make of the providence of God? What
practical atheists we often are in the conduct of our ordinary day! It
is a great thing to see God in the manna. It is a greater to see Him in
the fields. It is a great thing to see God in the miracle. It is a greater
to see Him in the usual. To waken in the dull morning and feel that
God is there; to go to our drudgery and have His presence; to live in
the faith that the hairs of our head are numbered and that not one
sparrow can fall without our Father, *that* is the mark of growing
trust in God. That was the doctrine of providence which Israel
learned when the manna ceased and the harvesting began. That is
the doctrine which was taught by Jesus, and in the might of which
He was so calm. And that is the doctrine which should be ours
tonight, when we have had in our hands today a piece of bread,
nothing unusual or extraordinary, yet rich in the tidings of redeeming love.[3]

And then—in closing—there is one other lesson which I love to
link with the ceasing of the manna. It is how God, as we advance in
life, brings us back to the food of long ago. Had there been any
manna down in Egypt? Had manna been Israel's food before the
Exodus? There were few now who could recall these days; yet corn,
not manna, had been the food of Egypt. And now the wanderers
come back to corn, to the old nurture of the storied past, yet all so
radiant now with love and mercy that the old has become new
forevermore. That was the path by which God led His people. He
brought them back to the old, and it was new. That is the path by
which God leads us all if we are in earnest to know and do His will.
We toil and we suffer and we play our part, and we feast on dew-
touched manna for a season; but the truths that we need to live by
and to die by are the commonplaces of the long ago. Do I speak to
any students here tonight who have come up as freshmen to the

---

2. to have regards or concern for
3. Preached on the evening of Communion Sunday.

University? My brother, I could almost envy you these glorious years of the manna just beginning. Take all advantage of them. Do not play the coward. Argue, discuss, follow the gleam bravely. But life is long and hard and full of tears and sin, and you will crave for the old commonplaces yet. Do not smile at that, as if it were out of date. Things timeless are never out of date. We have all had our manna-days, and we thank God for them; they were so full of wonder and delight. But life is stern, and sin is very terrible, and the manna has ceased and we are back to corn—back to our fathers' need of a Redeemer, back to the feet of an all-sufficient Christ.

Jesus answered him, I spake openly to the
world . . . and in secret have I said nothing
(John 18:20).

6

The Candor of Christ

In the revived interest which is felt today in the person and character of Jesus Christ, it is inevitable that close attention should be directed to His words. There are teachers whose life you can separate from their words, ignoring the one while you regard the other; but you never can create a gulf like that between the words and the character of Jesus. To His own mind, His sayings and His person were correlated in the most vital way. He carries over from one sphere to the other some of the richest blessings of discipleship. What the flower is to its deep-hidden root, what the rays of sunshine are to the sun, that is the oral teaching of our Lord to His gracious and unfathomable person.

Now among the attributes of our Redeemer's speech one which arrests attention is its candor. In our text our Lord lays claim to a great openness, and it is a claim which cannot be disputed. The whole impression made by the life of Jesus is that of a teacher who was frank and bold; of one who would not hesitate to speak, whatever the consequences to Himself might be; of one who rejoiced in liberty of utterance out of a heart that was full to overflowing, as a stream rejoices to make the meadows musical, when fed from the springs of the everlasting hills. There is many a reserved and silent man who has to be coaxed and wheedled into speech. There are those who are eloquent in high-strung moods but almost inaudible in common days. But the impression which Christ makes is not such; it is that of one to whom utterance was a joy, and whose words, out of unfathomed depths, welled over in the beauty of unpremeditated wisdom.

Of course this candor of our Lord and Master was always at the service of His love. It was the instrument of a pure and perfect sympathy which knew that there were seasons to be silent. No passion is so free of speech as love; none has the secret of such winning eloquence; yet love, which can unlock the dullest lips, is also mistress in the art of sealing them; and the perfect candor of our Redeemer's talk was ever subservient to that noblest love, which dares to speak when other lips are silent and to be silent when other voices speak. "I have yet many things to say to you," said Christ, "but ye cannot bear them now." New truths were welling up, seeking for utterance, yet remained unuttered at the behest of love. The time was coming when hearts would be established and able to bear the weight of revelation; but until then, in the judgment of the Master, to be candid was only to be cruel. There is a candor which is the child of ignorance, for fools rush in where angels fear to tread.[1] There is a candor which betrays the bitter heart, for it speaks the truth, but does not speak in love. But the candor of Jesus goes hand in hand with reticence, and both look up to catch their inspiration from the most loving and sympathetic eyes that ever beamed upon a sinful world.

We may trace this candor of our Lord in many spheres—in His treatment, for instance, of those who came to Him. He scorned to disguise the truth about the future from those who sought an entrance to His kingdom. Think of that scribe of whom we read tonight and who came to Him bubbling over with enthusiasm. "Lord, I will follow Thee whithersoever Thou goest," was his eager and excited cry. Now had Jesus said to him, "I welcome thee—thou art a child of Abraham indeed," none would have doubted that the text was genuine. There are seasons of dejection and depression when any disciple seems better than none at all. There are times when the loyalty even of shallow hearts is very precious to a suspected leader. And was not this man a scribe—a learned person—one of the class who were bitter foes to Christ; and would not his allegiance, once secured, be more important than that of twenty fishermen? All

---

1. From "An Essay on Man" by Alexander Pope (1688–1744), English poet.

that might have weighed with other leaders; it was light as gossamer to Jesus Christ. His only care was to be frank and true to a soul that did not know what it was doing. And so the word of welcome was not spoken; but instead, a word as sad as it was searching, "Foxes have holes, and the birds of the air have nests, but the Son of Man hath not where to lay His head." Christ will have no disciple on false pretenses. He issues no rosy prospectus of His kingdom. He never hides, from those who wish to serve Him, that right in the path of the future is a cross. And this is the candor not of indifference but of love, which shrinks from the least appearance of deception and will have no man say in bitter moments that he was tricked unto discipleship by guile.

Again we note the candor of our Lord in the charges which He hurled against the Pharisees. In the whole range of human utterance there are no more deadly or awful accusations. "Woe unto you, scribes and Pharisees"—how dreadful is the reiteration of that doom, like the recurring mutterings of thunder over a meadow land of summer beauty. Most of us have had moments when we wished that these dark and dreadful words had not been spoken. They are so hard to reconcile with love and with that gentleness of Christ which makes us great.[2] Yet all these charges, so fearless and so frank and so utterly regardless of all consequence, were part of the battle which Jesus Christ was fighting on behalf of misguided and downtrodden men. There is a deep sense in which it was Christ's candor that brought Him at last to His death upon the cross. Had He refrained from His speech against the Pharisees, He might have escaped the fury of their hate. But for Christ such silence would have been betrayal of the very cause that He had come to battle for, and therefore to be silent was impossible. It was not because the Pharisees despised Him that Jesus flashed on them in splendid anger. Our Lord was sublimely and superbly heedless of indignities that were offered to Himself. But it was because they marred the name of God and sullied the fair features of religion and changed the happy service of the Father into a burden too heavy to be borne.

Now there are times in every life when it takes a certain courage to be quiet. To every man and woman there come seasons when the path of duty is the path of silence. All that is basest in us bids us speak, for there is a candor that is the child of hell; but all that is noblest in us checks our speech, lest to someone we do irreparable harm. But re-

2. Psalm 18:35

member if it takes courage to be quiet, it also may call for courage to be frank. To speak the word that we know ought to be spoken may rob the eyes of sleep through a long night. And when the heart is sensitive and tender and shrinks instinctively from causing pain, the duty of candor becomes doubly difficult. All that ought to be borne in mind when we consider the candor of our Lord. No one could charge Him with being hard or cold. He was gentle-hearted and exquisitely sensitive. Yet frankly and fearlessly, not in a blind fury but as a duty that had to be discharged, He swept the Pharisees with withering scorn.

Again we note the candor of our Lord in saying that there were things He did not know. Think, for example, of the account He gives of the final coming of the Son of Man. It is a wonderful and awful picture, fresh from a heart that had a vision of it. Clothed in the imagery of the ancient prophets, it is yet something mightier than the prophets dreamed of. But immediately, having described that hour, our Savior adds that He does not know that hour—"Of that day and hour knoweth no man, no, not the Son, but the Father." To me there is nothing startling whatever in the mere fact of such an ignorance. Was it not part of that humiliation to which our Lord had voluntarily stooped? Surely the humiliation would have been incomplete had the mind of Jesus been excluded from it by still retaining, in all its height and depth, the perfection of knowledge which is God's. It is not the ignorance that is so wonderful. It is the frank confession of that ignorance. It is the way in which Christ, who made such mighty claims, said to His followers, "I do not know." And it seems to me that such a splendid candor, with all the inevitable risks it brought, is a mightier argument for trusting Christ than many which the theologians adduce. When a man who is a master in some science says to me candidly, "I do not know," I am always readier to trust that man when he unlocks the riches of his knowledge. And so when Jesus, quietly and frankly, says to His own, "I do not know that hour," somehow it makes me readier to believe Him when He speaks of duty, of heaven, and of God. People who only know a little are the people who are afraid to show their ignorance. Those who know most are always the most ready to tell you frankly what they do not know. And so when Jesus Christ declares His ignorance and does so freely and without compulsion, I feel I am in the presence of a Master whose statements can be absolutely trusted. There is a lack of candor in some Christian teachers which is utterly alien from the Master's spirit. If they would only tell us what they mean, it would be easier to know what they don't mean. It is not the mark of the greatest and the best to be tortuous and "irrecoverably dark."[3] In all the greatest there is a certain candor akin to the simplicity of Christ.

Then the last sphere in which I note this frankness is in His relationship with His disciples. With an open and overflowing heart Christ gave Himself to the friendship of His own. It was said of Cardinal Newman, by one who ought to know, that he had the capacity for wholehearted friendship. It is not such a common capacity as we imagine, though the name of friend be often on our lips. But certainly it was possessed by Jesus and exercised in such fullness toward His own that life and death and love and pain and joy were different ever afterward to them. Now one of the marks of the capacity for friendship is the power to give oneself in happy confidence. There is the opening toward a friend of many a door that is fast barred in the presence of the world. Heart goes out to heart in simple trust, and mind is kindled at the touch of mind, and the reserve and coldness which the world necessitates are quite forgotten in that tender intimacy. No man can ever hope to be a friend who looks on candor as a doubtful virtue. There is no friendship worthy of the name for the man who wraps his nature in reserve. And the very fact that Christ was such a friend that His friendship made all the difference to the twelve is the best proof, if proof were needed, of the glorious frankness of the Savior. Read over again the Gospel of St. John, which is so full of His converse with His own. Compare and contrast it with the other Gospels, which are the record of His public ministry. Do that, and you will speedily discover how frank was the self-disclosure of our Lord, when in the company of those who trusted Him, and whose hearts "burned within them while He spoke."

In closing may I say a single word about the response this should evoke from us? Charles Dickens in *Nicholas Nickleby*[4] says this: "Among men who have any sound and sterling qualities, there is nothing so contagious as pure openness of heart." Christ, then, opens His heart to you; will you not respond by opening yours to Him? Christ wants to deal with you in perfect frankness; will you not be frank and honest in return? Make no concealment. Do not excuse yourself. Trust Him, and tell Him all the story. A confidence like that He always honors with a blessing which is heaven begun.

---

3. From "Sonnet: To the Nightingale" by Milton.
4. Chapter 35

I returned, and saw under the sun, that the
race is not to the swift, nor the battle to the
strong (Eccl. 9:11).

7

The Race Not to the Swift

I ask you to note the first words of our text. The writer begins by
saying "I returned." Now what does he mean by that, and where had
he been, and why does he tell us he came back again? He means that
there had been a time when he sat in his house with a hot and angry
heart. He had thought it a shame that some should be so swift and that
others should be so beautiful or strong. What was the use of striving
for the prize when some of the athletes were so unfairly handicapped?
It was a cruel world, unbalanced and unjust, and his heart was in
revolt against its ordering. Then he went out into the world's highways. He moved up and down among the haunts of men. He ceased
to theorize and set himself to watch what was actually happening
upon the stage of action; and then, with a mind furnished with large
experience, he came home to meditate upon it all. "And I returned,
and saw under the sun"—things wore a different complexion now.
Men might be swift, but they did not always win. Armies might be
strong, but they did not always triumph. There were incalculable
powers abroad—balancing, adjusting, compensating—so that turn
where one would in human affairs, there were unexpected and dramatic issues. Now if you like, says the writer, you may call that
chance; or you may take it from the other side and call it God. But

whatever you call it, the certain fact remains that the rearranging and revising power is there. And so, says the preacher, I came home again, a wiser, a humbler, and a happier man, for I had seen that the race is not to the swift nor is the battle to the strong.

Tonight, then, I shall try to illustrate that truth and then to show the moral values of it. And in the first place do as this writer did, and look with your own eyes upon your own environment. One of the favorite words of Dr. John Brown[1]—the gentle author of *Rab and His Friends*—one of the words that was often on his lips was the word *unexpectedness*. And as we look on the men whom we have known since childhood and whose lives we have watched unrolling in the years, there are very few of us within this house who cannot discern that unexpected element. Was there not one in our schoolboy days who was our hero? Were we not certain he was going to be famous? He was so clever, so brilliant, did with such perfect ease the things that we laboriously struggled with! But the years have passed with their discipline and chastening, and he has disappointed all our hopes; and some dull head, that once we might have jeered at, has been lifting himself up bravely toward the crown. Now I do not investigate the causes of that failure; that does not lie within our present scope. It may have been instability or secret sin or lack of the master-key of courage. But whatever it be, like the preacher we return, taught by the years and what our eyes have witnessed, and we feel how true it is of our own circle, that the race is not to the swift nor the battle to the strong.

Or once again, widening our view a little, we may trace our text through all kinds of achievement. You have but to think of the books by which we live or of those lives of thought and action which are our richest heritage, to be face to face with that incalculable element which lies in the divine method of surprise. Would you not expect the best work to be done by those who possess (as we think) every advantage? If a man is to write a great book or a great poem, must he not have leisure and libraries and health and strength? So we imagine, as the preacher did, and then we face the facts and we return, taught by our survey that there is a power abroad which travels counter to our expectations. We think of Homer,[2] and learn that he was blind; of Epictetus,[3] and he was a slave. We think of Amos, and he was a herdsman; of the

---

1. Sir John Brown (1810–1882), English essayist and medical doctor.

2. Homer (8th century B.C.), Greek epic poet and reputed author of the *Iliad* and *Odyssey*.

3. Epictetus (c. A.D. 60–120), Stoic philosopher.

Apostle John, he was a fisherman. We think of Bunyan,[4] a tinker and imprisoned. We think of Burns[5] with his hand upon the plow. Where is your leisure there, and where your libraries—where is your atmosphere of cultured ease? There is a hand at work we cannot stay, and it hath exalted those of low degree. I stood, a week or two ago among the statues in Westminster Abbey,[6] lingering, with many awakened memory, amid the long shadows of the Poets' Corner.[7] And does that storied corner speak of riches? Here are "a company of glorious paupers." Of learning? Little Latin and less Greek. Of strength? Count up the number who were dead at forty. It speaks of struggle against tremendous odds, of poverty and suffering and despair; yet these have won their triumph on the field and carried off the laurel in the race. So I returned, as every man returns, feeling how inscrutable is providence; how often those who have everything have nothing, and those who seem to have nothing gain the crown. So "I returned, and saw under the sun, that the race is not to the swift nor the battle to the strong."

Again, our text has singular significance in that universal search, the search for happiness. It is not those who have most to make them happy who always prove themselves the happy people. There are people of whom we instinctively say, "Well, he should be happy. He has everything that this world can offer him. He has health and money and friends and a sweet home, and he has not a care or worry in the world." Yet sometimes when we get to know such people, we find them not so happy as we thought; and men who are burdened and battling with a thousand ills have more of the laughter and of the song than they. I wonder if in all the homes of Philippi there were any such praiseful men as Paul and Silas. Philippi was a noble and luxurious city, rich in the arts that minister to pleasure. Yet if you want to find the gladdest hearts in Philippi, you must leave its palaces and get you to its dungeon, where, beaten and bruised and in the stocks at midnight, two aliens are so happy that they sing. We talk about the eager race for riches; but at the heart of it, it is a race for happiness. We speak of the grim battle to succeed; it is really the battle to be happy. And if one thing is certain, when we return again from looking in the eyes of men and women, it is that that race is not always to the swift nor is that battle always to the strong.

---

4. John Bunyan (1628–1688), English Nonconformist preacher and author of *Pilgrim's Progress*.

5. Robert Burns (1759–1796), Scottish poet.

6. Gothic church and national shrine in London, England.

7. Poets' Corner—south transept of Westminster Abbey where some of England's great poets are buried.

And this is conspicuously true of Jesus Christ, the Man of Sorrows and acquainted with grief. I like sometimes to contrast the Man of Nazareth with the emperor who was reigning then, Tiberius. Tiberius was the most powerful of living men, the ruler of all that was fairest in the world. There was no control to his power, no limit to his wealth, no check or barrier upon his pleasures. On one of the most enchanting spots of earth he chose his home—on a lovely island with a delicious climate. Does not the thought of that conjure up happiness? Would not you be happy if all that were yours? Yet Pliny,[8] who ought to know something of the matter, calls him *tristissimus ut constat hominum*[9]—confessedly the most gloomy of mankind. Now think of Christ, with nowhere to lay His head, despised and rejected, jeered at, crucified. Hearken to His words about "My joy"—"My peace, that the world cannot give and cannot take away." Who wins in that race for happiness and peace? Is it the mighty Caesar or the rejected Christ? The race is not always to the swift, nor is the battle always to the strong.[10]

And then our text applies to the spiritual life, for not many wise, not many mighty are called. God hath chosen the weak things of the world to bring to nought those that are strong in battle. Recall the Pharisees, those guardians of the past, those men whose whole profession was religion. Trained in the law and looking for Messiah, will not they be the first to press into the kingdom? Yet, "Woe unto you, Pharisees and scribes," says Christ, "swift though you seem, the race is not for you." It is for weeping harlots like the Magdalene and penitent and adoring publicans like Matthew. I know no sphere in human life where the element of unexpectedness so largely enters as in the sphere that we call spiritual and in the movements and changes of the soul. When I was in college we had great revival times associated with the name of Henry Drummond,[11] and as I look back on these glad and golden days, one feature of them stands out very clearly. Some of the men who had every advantage and who came out of pious and God-fearing homes went on their way utterly uninfluenced by the grace of God that was so freely working. And some who came right out into the light and have been walking in the light

---

8. Pliny (A.D. 23–79), Roman naturalist, encyclopedist, and writer. Pliny the younger (A.D. 62?–c113), Roman writer, statesman, and orator.

9. "the most sorrowful, melancholy, and unvarying man"

10. I think I owe the suggestion of this contrast to a passage in some book by Canon Farrar.

11. Henry Drummond (1851–1897), Scottish clergyman and writer.

from that day forward were the last men you would have ever looked for, if you had known them as their fellow-students did. There is not a minister but could tell you the same story; there is not a mission-worker but would echo it—some from whom brightest things were hoped, proving intractable; and some who seemed hard as granite, yielding joyfully. So we return from service for the Lord with larger experience of how the battle goes, taught by the tale of trophy and of failure that the race is not to the swift nor the battle to the strong.

And now in closing let me suggest to you some of the moral values of this truth, and first, it is mighty to keep us from discouragement and to cheer us when the lights are burning dim. Thank God, we can say in our weakness, I may still win my crown, for the battle is not always to the strong. You are not swift nor clever nor remarkable? But the race is not always to the swift. You are not gifted with unusual strength? But the battle is not always to the strong. It gives a chance to mediocre people, to commonplace and undistinguished thousands, when above all might and brilliance is a power that has a way of working to unexpected ends. "Whatsoever thy hand findeth to do, do it with all thy might." Do not say, "Ah, if I had the gifts of so and so." A little gift, in the hand of a great God, may work for mightier issues than you think.

Then it is meant to wean us from all pride and to keep us watchful, humble, and dependent. Is there anyone here of swift and subtle intellect? Remember that the race is not always to the swift. I put no premium on mediocrity. I honor talent wherever it is found. I love to meet with bright and brilliant men. I love to look upon strengths in any form. But if you are swift, do not despise the slow; if you are strong, do not condemn the weak. It is a strange world, rich in dramatic touches, and the battle is not always to the strong.

Lastly, it clears the ground for God and leaves a space to recognize Him in. If the strongest were sure of triumph in every battle, there would be little room on the field for the divine. Whose is the hand that in the race of life so often wreathes the chaplet for the slow? Whose is the arm that so upholds the weak that after the strife theirs is the cry of victory? "There's a divinity that shapes our ends, rough hew them how we will."[12] So we return, we who were once so blind, with eyes that have been opened to see God, and now we know that just because *He* reigns, the battle is not always to the strong.

---

12. From *Hamlet* by Shakespeare.

Some say that Thou art . . . Elias; and
others, Jeremias (Matt. 16:14).

8

Elijah or Jeremiah

It is of the deepest interest to discover what was the common
impression about Jesus, and in this report conveyed by the disciples
we get a hint of the utmost value. "Whom do men say that I am?"
said Jesus; and the answer was, "Some say John the Baptist; but
others—and probably the greater number—think Thou art Elijah or
Jeremiah come to earth again." Now there are many interesting
suggestions in these answers; but one of them to my mind overtops
all the others. Did you ever think of the vast difference there was
between the characters of Elijah and Jeremiah? Yet some said about
Christ, "This is Elijah," and others said, "No, it is Jeremiah." If you
read again the page of the Old Testament, you will appreciate the
gulf between the two. The one is ardent, enthusiastic, fierce sometimes. The other is the prophet of the tender heart and tears. And the
remarkable thing is that the common people should have taken
these types, which are so wide apart, and should have found in both
the character of Christ. In other words, the impression which Jesus
made was that of a complex, inclusive personality. You could not
exhaust Him by a single prophet. It took the range of the greatest to
portray His character. And I want this evening to try to bring before
you some of these qualities of different natures, which harmonize
so perfectly and wonderfully in the human nature of our Lord.

First, then, I am arrested in Christ's character by the perfect
union of mastery and charm.[1] It is one of the rarest things in the
world to find the masterful man possessed of the indefinable quality
of charm. There are some people born to be obeyed, and there are
other people born to be loved; but it is very rarely that the compelling nature, in the language of Scripture, is "altogether lovely."
Think of the masterful men whom you have known; the men whose
distinguishing attribute was power; the men who never insisted on
obedience yet somehow or other always were obeyed; the men who
were very quiet and very strong. Such men are always needed in the
commonwealth—such men are always secretly admired; but it is
very seldom, in this curious world, that such authoritative men are
loved. What they lack is the indefinable quality of charm. They can
master everything except the heart. They appeal to all that is strong
and virile in us. They do *not* appeal to the imagination. And it is
strange what a deal the people will forgive and how they will cover
up a hundred failings in the man who appeals to their imagination.

Now when we turn to Christ, the first thing we observe is that the
mark of His character is power. Here is no sentimental dreamer from
the hills; here is a regal, authoritative man. Read over His life in the
Gospels once again, and mark how often that word "power" occurs.
"His word was with power," says Luke. "The kingdom comes with
power," says Mark. "The multitude glorified God who had given
such power unto men," says Matthew. We are quite wrong in saying
about Jesus that the first impression which He made was that of
gentleness—the first impression which He made was one of power.
He spoke with authority, and not as one of the scribes. And why did
men leave all when he said, "Follow Me"? And in the garden when
He was betrayed and said to them, "I am He"—why did the rabble
shrink and fall away? There is something so magnificent in that—in
the sheer power of that defenseless manhood—that I defy any painter
to portray it. Yet look at the little children how they came to Him and
nestled without a tremor in His arms. And think of Peter by the Sea
of Galilee, "Lord, Thou knowest that I *love* Thee." Some men are
born to be obeyed, some to be loved; but Jesus preeminently was
born for both. That is why people said, "Lo, here is Elijah," and

---

1. For this address, both in substance and illustration, I would acknowledge
my deep indebtedness to Professor Peabody's book, *Jesus Christ and the Christian Character*. I know few books of recent years more stimulating to the preacher than those of Professor Peabody of Harvard.

others, "No, it is Jeremiah." All that had marked the noblest of the prophets was harmonized and reconciled in Him—untold authority, infinite sensibility, a will that would not swerve, a tender heart, the union of mastery and charm.

Again, I am arrested in Christ's character by the union of remoteness and accessibility. There is something in Christ that always suggests distance. There is much in Christ that tells us He is near. Now there are many people who convey the impression of remoteness, though none in the same way as Jesus did. There is the man who is absorbed in some great work, for instance; and we feel when we meet him that he moves apart. And there is a certain type of the religious spirit that is so cold and so icily immaculate that a poor sinner, like the rich man in hell, sees what a gulf there is between him and Abraham. What you feel is, when men are so remote, that you must not trouble them with your small matters. You must not look to them for the sweet word of sympathy. You must not expect them to bother about *you*. They lift themselves apart like some high Alp, which catches the morning but is always snow-clad; while we poor mortals with hearts so weak, so warm must struggle along in the valleys as we may.

Brethren, there never lived on earth a man who so impressed men with his remoteness as did Christ. "Depart from me, for I am a sinful man, O Lord," was how it all appealed to Simon Peter. You remember how Milton[2] in his "Hymn of the Nativity" says, "Kings sat still with awful eye, as if they surely knew their sovran[3] Lord was by!" and I tell you there are a hundred touches in the gospel that confirm that impression of the incarnate Lord. It is the height of childishness for any gospel-student to say that Jesus was just a genial socialist. "Gentlemen," said Napoleon, "I know men, and you may take my word for it, this is more than man."[4] For He stood apart; men felt He was remote; there was the touch of the faraway about this figure. Some said Elias, and others Jeremiah; no one said, "A genial, pleasant neighbor." The strange thing is that though Christ thus stood remote, men should have come to Him with every worry. "Come unto Me," and they came from every rank—from the lady of the court to the poor reprobate. And He who stood so far apart that He could say, "Thy sins are forgiven thee, go in peace"; yet stood so near that there was not a sorrow He could not appre-

2. John Milton (1608–1674), English poet, author of *Paradise Lost*.
3. sovereign
4. Napoleon I (1769–1821), French general, emperor of France 1804–1815.

ciate and understand. Some said Elias, that lone figure, standing apart from the surge and flow of Israel. And some said Jeremiah— tenderhearted, whose tears were a river for his people's sorrow. And both were wrong yet both supremely right, for Elias and Jeremiah both were here. Christ was far more lonely than the one and far more sympathetic than the other.

Once more I am arrested in Christ's character by the union of enthusiasm and tranquillity. His feelings were often powerfully stirred, yet the whole impression is one of profound peace. There are men who can walk unmoved through a vast crowd. When Christ saw a crowd, He was touched with compassion always. There are men who can stand beside a grave emotionless; by the grave of Lazarus, Jesus wept. There are men who can view all manner of iniquity and never lose a moment's peace about it; but Jesus, in a mighty surge of indignation, drove out the buyers and sellers from the temple. Clearly, this is no cold, phlegmatic nature. There is nothing of the steeled heart of the Stoic here. Here is a man whose eye will flash sometimes, whose soul can be roused into a glow of passion. And yet the one impression of the whole is not that of an eager, strained unrest; the impression of the whole life of Jesus is that of an unutterable peace. It is very easy to be cold yet calm; to be uninterested, unimpassioned, and so tranquil. It is very easy to deaden down the feelings, until a man has made a solitude and called it peace. But the abiding wonder about Christ is this, that He had an ardent, eager, enthusiastic heart yet breathed such a deep, such a superb tranquillity, that men instinctively felt He was at rest.

Then, in closing and most notable of all, there is the union of abnegation and appreciation. I regret using such ungainly words, but I know no others that so express my meaning. What is the last word in the ideal of Jesus—is it asceticism, or is it joy? Let me show you in a word how Christendom has leaned at different times to different answers.

Think, then, on the one hand of medieval painters who have portrayed for us the man of Nazareth. It is not the Christ who considered the lilies whom they paint. It is the Christ of agony and shame. You know that figure kneeling in the garden. You know that face with its awful look of agony. You know these hands with the blood dropping from them, and St. Dominic[5] looking upward with enraptured eyes. And even where the suffering is shrouded by an art as exquisite as it is perfect, you know that the appeal of all such art

---

5. St. Dominic (1170–1221), Spanish priest, founder of Dominican order.

is, "Come, and let us mourn with Him awhile." It is not joy that animates these pictures; it is a calm and holy acquiescence. It is not intense delight in the glad world; it is unquestioning acceptance of the will of God. He has given up everything, this Christ, to die for men, and the last word of that art is abnegation.

And then I turn to some modern lives of Christ, and I seem to be moving in a different world. I turn to Renan,[6] to Zangwill,[7] or to Dawson, and I hardly recognize the painter's figure. He is entranced with the vision of the divine life, says Renan, and He gives Himself with delight to its expression. He is the incarnation of the spirit of joy, says Dawson.[8] And Mr. Zangwill, in his *Dreamers of the Ghetto*, says, "I give the Jews a Christ they can accept now; the lover of warm life and the warm sunlight, and all that is fresh and beautiful and pure." Is this the medieval sufferer with the blood-drops and with the crown of thorns? Is this glad poet with His glowing cheek the pallid figure of medieval paintings? It is not suffering that is the keynote here. It is positive, intense, and simple joy. It is not abnegation of the world; the keynote is appreciation.

"Some said Elias, others Jeremiah"—have we not here another echo of such judgments? The wonder of Jesus is not this *or* that; the wonder of Jesus is this *and* that together. There is a joy that has no room in it for sacrifice; it is too selfish, too sensuous, and too shallow. There is a sacrifice that is absolutely joyless, without a gleam of the sunshine on its cross. But Christ was happy as a child in this green world, because not a sparrow could fall without His Father; yet He gave up everything and died on Calvary, that guilty men and women might be saved. In the deepest of all senses Christ renounced the world and trampled all its glory underfoot. The first condition of following in His train was that one should lead the life of self-denial. Yet he who so followed Him was never deadened to the call of lovely or delightful things; he was led into a world where birds were singing and which was beautiful with the lilies of the field. That is why in Christ there is neither Jew nor Greek. All are united in that wonderful character. That is why you and I can never say, "He was Elias," or, "He was Jeremiah." Embracing both—all that was best in both—and all that is highest and fairest in humanity; we fall before Him and reply with Peter, "Thou art the Christ, the Son of the living God."

6. Ernest Renan (1823–1892), French philologist, historian, and critic.

7. Israel Zangwill (1865–1926), English novelist and playwright.

8. William James Dawson (1854–1928), English minister and writer, *The Man Christ Jesus*, p. 82.

Except a corn of wheat fall into the ground
and die, it abideth alone: but if it die it
bringeth forth much fruit (John 12:24).

9

The Cross and Nature

At the beginning of the summertime I have been in the habit of speaking on the religious aspects of the world of nature, for there are few of us whose thoughts do not travel in that direction when we waken to find ourselves in June again. In the South, where the sun is warm even at Christmas time, there is no surprise and delight about the summer. It is just the same as winter, only a little hotter and generally a little more uncomfortable. But in the North here it is far different from that. Between November and June there is a world of contrast. The one is bare and bleak and icy and disheveled. The other is fresh and beautiful, green-leafed, long-grassed. And probably it is this change, so great and striking that the blindest eye cannot but observe it, that has made the northern nations so responsive to the wonder and the beauty of the world. They say that one effect of death has been to heighten enormously the worth of life. I think that is true not alone of the death of persons but also of the death of summertime. There are countries where summer never dies, and there the summer is but lightly recked[1] of. It is here, where we forecast the grave of winter, that we love and cherish the summer when it comes. Tonight, then, in accordance with my

---

1. regarded, taken heed of

custom at this season, I wish to turn your thoughts to the subject of the summer. More especially I wish to speak about the Cross of Christ in its relationship to the world of nature.

Now at first glance no two things could seem more different than the cross of Calvary and the summer-world. The night is not more different from the day—the sea is not more different from the land—than the cross is from the green fields of June. On the one hand you have sadness and farewell; on the other, you have the joy of teeming life. On the one hand you have a crown of thorns; on the other, a chaplet of a thousand flowers. On the one hand you have a scene of agony; on the other, the singing voices of the birds. On the one hand, "My God, My God, why hast Thou forsaken Me?" on the other, a world that throbs with the divine. No contrast could be sharper or more terrible. One could hardly conceive of a kinship between the two. To take the Cross and intrude it on the summer seems like intruding a deathbed on a feast. And so there are many, in these long June days, who are apt to feel they are out of touch with Calvary, just because they are in touch—and love to be so— with the color and wealth and music of the world.

But there is one service which science often renders, and that is to reveal most unexpected kinships. She brings together into the closest union things that seem different as day and night. A child goes out into the fields and gathers buttercups, and then in the garden she plucks a bunch of columbines, and the two to her seem absolutely different in color, form, arrangement, everything. Yet ask a botanist, and he will tell you at once, that in spite of all that may mislead the child, columbine and buttercup are next-of-kin. That is what science has done in *little* things. It is also what she has done in greater spheres. So far from being antagonistic to religion, she has rendered it by her faithful toil one mighty service. For at the heart of nature, where the childish eye finds nothing but light and liberty and song, she has discovered the shadow of the Cross.

I would remark in passing that this close kinship between the Cross and the world of outward nature is something that we should expect to find when we remember the life of Jesus Christ on earth. Our Lord loved nature; He dwelt much in nature. He was always at home among its hills and fields. It is no accident that His first sermon was delivered under the blue sky and where the breeze was blowing. He did not shun the homes and haunts of men. He did not avoid the noisy and close synagogue. It is one of the beautiful things about that life that it was so perfect in its balance.

Yet never over this green and gladsome earth did there walk one
in deeper sympathy with summer, than the Savior who loved the
freshness of the dawn and the sleep that is among the lonely hills.
Now why was He here? Not merely to live, but to *die*—willingly
and deliberately to die. The shadow of the Cross was on His heart.
He came to be crucified for sinful men. And if nature, with all her
wealth and song, be utterly out of sympathy with Calvary, I cannot
understand how Jesus loved her and moved among her silences at
peace. No man is ever in living touch with nature if the master-
passion of his life defies her. If the end to which a man is making
is *un*natural, no cloud nor sunset will speak its thought to him.
And so if the Cross which was the goal of Christ was out of
harmony with flower and bird, to me the companionship that Jesus
found in nature becomes the greatest riddle of His life. Of course
you may say that Jesus went to nature not to find kinship but to
escape the Cross. But to say *that* is to brand Him as a coward, and
even His enemies make no such charge. No man takes up a great
life's work and then spends the best hours of every day trying to
forget it. To do that is unworthy of a hero—how utterly
unbelievable of Christ! It was not to *forget* the Cross He went to
nature, but because He felt that the Cross was in the summer and
that in every lily of the field there was something which was akin
to Calvary.

But you may naturally ask me what I mean when I say we have
been wakened to the cross in nature. In answer, let me direct you to
some facts.

For instance, we have been wakened to see in nature a mighty
and persistent power to save. Explain it how you will, there is a
spirit abroad that is determined to seek and save the lost. A million
years may be spent upon some touch that is hidden away in the
tiniest of weeds, and all to give that weed—that any hoof may
crush—a better chance in its battle against death. Did you ever
think of nature's prodigality? Did you ever ask yourself seriously
what it meant? Did you ever wonder that in a single beech-tree
there are seeds enough to line a hundred avenues? It means that the
spirit which is abroad in summer is willing to lavish anything and
everything rather than let its struggling children die. "It is not the
will of your Father which is in heaven that one of these little ones
should perish." There is not a flower, not a fern nor moss, but
carries that message to the hearing ear. And *that* spirit, which counts
no cost too great if only the life of the feeblest may be saved—that

is the very spirit of the Cross. The Cross is a scene of boundless prodigality—of a love that deemed no sacrifice too great. The Cross is God's gift of all that was most dear to Him that you and I might be empowered to live. And it is the foregleams of this passionate earnestness to save, with which the story of summertime is full, that bring it into unison with Calvary.

Again, we have been wakened now to see the struggle that lies behind the beauty of the world. The world of nature was not always beautiful; it has risen to beauty through the strife of ages. Could anything be more peaceful than a summer evening when the wind is hushed and every leaf is still? Could anything be more eloquent of rest, more full of the beauty that is a joy forever? Yet we know now that behind that brooding calm, which like a mantle enwraps the world of twilight, is one of the grimmest tales of war and death that ever was written for mankind to read. Peace, perfect peace? Yes, there is peace in nature, yet in the making of it has been war. Rest— in the bosom of the summer world—yet behind the rest, a travail and an agony. When once we have learned that secret of the summer, we are not far from the cross upon the hill. What does the Savior say to us tonight?—"Come unto Me, and I will give you rest." And we have companied with men who had that rest and in whose looks was the beatitude of peace. Yet ask these men what is behind it all—behind that calm as of a summer evening—and they will tell you of blood-drops and a crown of thorns, and of a breast that once was pierced upon the tree.

And then again we have been wakened to this, that nature is full of shadows of self-sacrifice. The deepest note of the summer is not savagery; the deepest note is sacrifice of self. Every flower that fades is dying that it may live. Every bird that guards its young is on the lines of Calvary. Not on the ruined altar but on the living cross does the sparrow mystically find herself a nest. "Except a corn of wheat fall into the ground and die, it abideth alone: but if it die it bringeth forth much fruit." Who impressed that law upon the seed and wrote it on the beauty of every flower that faded? Surely the meaning of it all is this, that the world is built upon redemption's lines and that through the universe runs, like a thread of gold, the spirit that came to its glory in the Passion. If self were the final chord in summer's music, it could never be brought into harmony with Calvary. Then would there be, between the Cross and nature, such discord as none but devils could delight in. But when, through the leafy wealth of every June, I see in death the avenue of life, I turn to a crucified Savior and adore Him. His Cross does not contradict, it crowns, the summer.

And now in closing I want to say one word. It is about the joy we feel in summertime. There are men who have said to me, "I cannot be glad in nature any more, since I have learned the story of its struggle." "Once," they have said, "I was happy in the world; it was so beautiful, so restful, and so innocent; but now there has fallen a shadow on its peace, and nature will never be glad to me again." With that mood I deeply sympathize. There was a time when it clouded all the world for me. I could not listen to a singing bird without the intrusion of unkindly thoughts. But I have learned that one may recall that gladness and find it stronger because broadbased on fact, when once in the shadow on the heart of nature, the eye has seen the shadow of the Cross. "Rejoice in the Lord, and again I say, Rejoice." Do we rejoice in Christ less because He died? Is not Christian joy unfailing and unspeakable because at the very roots of it is Calvary? And so I turn again to the sweet world of June, with open eyes for its secret and its sorrow, to find it fairer than in the days of childhood, because the mystery of Christ is there.

Woman, why weepest thou?
(from John 20:11–18).

10

Love and Grief

In this beautiful and ever memorable incident there are three things upon which I wish to dwell. The first is Mary's grief; the second is Mary's love; and the third is the revelation of the Lord to Mary.

Let me speak, then, upon the grief of Mary, trying to make plain to you the greatness of that grief; and the first glimpse we get into its deeps is that Mary shows no wonder at the angels. At all the crises of the life of Christ we read of angels. We read of them at His birth, His temptation, and His agony. At these great moments His attendant bodyguard breaks through the veil, as it were, and becomes visible. And now in this great hour of hard-won victory, when death, the last great enemy, is beaten, there is a vision of angels in the tomb. There are two of them, in the tenderness of God, who would not send one alone to a dark sepulcher. They are clothed in white, the livery of heaven; they are seated, as in the calm of glory. Yet Mary, stooping down and peering in and catching a glimpse of these beings more than mortal, has not a fear and scarce a thought to give them, she is so brokenhearted for her Lord. There is nothing more absorbing than great grief. It banishes fear, surprise, dismay, astonishment. And from the utter absence of all such feelings here, we learn how terrible was Mary's grief.

The same intensity is manifest again when we notice how her grief embraced her world. Turning round in the dim dawn she saw a man, and she supposed that it had been the gardener. Now she had never seen that man before; he was a stranger to her and she to him. The circle that he moved in was not hers; he had his wife and children, his home and joys and sorrows. Yet she offers no explanation or apology, never mentions the name of Christ, just talks of *Him*—her grief is so overpowering that she cannot conceive that others should remain indifferent in her sorrow. I think that many of us have had times when our feeling was akin to that of Mary. In seasons of overwhelming sorrow—when the golden bowl is broken—the noisy life out in the streets is like an insult. It is incredible how others should be laughing and going about their work with eager hearts, when for us there is not a star within the welkin[1] and not a sound of music in the lute. Now of course that is an unreasonable mood, and we soon outgrow it if we are strong in God. But whether reasonable or unreasonable, it is human, one sign and symbol of overwhelming grief. And it is when we see Mary so absorbed that everyone she meets must know her sorrow, that we realize her womanly despair at the loss of her Savior and her Lord.

Then, too, her grief had made her blind. That also reveals the depth of her dismay. She heard the sound of a footfall, and there was Jesus standing, but Mary did not know that it was Jesus. Now there were many things to prevent that recognition; there was the dim and dusky light of early morning. There was the change that had passed upon the form of Christ now that He was risen in triumph from the grave. But the deepest cause was not in the morning light; the deepest cause was not in the face of Jesus; the deepest cause was in the heart of Mary. I have heard mourners gathered at a funeral say afterward, "I could not tell you who was there." All the great passions in their full intensity have got a certain blinding power about them. But neither love nor hate nor jealousy nor anger is more effectual in sealing up the eyes than is the pressure of overwhelming grief. So she turned herself round when she heard the quiet footfall. And Jesus was there, and she knew not it was He. Does that tell you that Jesus Christ was changed? It tells me also that Mary was brokenhearted.

And the strange thing is that had she only known it, the cause of her grief was to be the joy of ages. It was for an absent Lord that she was weeping, yet on that absence Christendom is built. "They

---

1. the sky

have taken away my Lord," said Mary; "let me but find His body and I shall be happy." But supposing she had found it and been happy, have you ever thought what that would have involved?—no resurrection, no sending of the Spirit, no gospel, no Christendom, no heaven. And so I learn that in our deepest griefs may lie the secret of our richest joys, and that there may be "a budding morrow in midnight."[2] It is better to go to the house of mourning than to the house of mirth. That does not mean it is better to be melancholy. The evangel of Christ is tidings of great joy, and no one had such a right to be glad as a true Christian. It means that, like Mary, in our sorest grief we may light on that which all the world's a-seeking; and that everything may be radiant ever after, because of the one thing that caused our tears.

So far, then, on the depth of Mary's grief. Now let us turn to the depth of Mary's love. And how intensely she loved may be most surely gathered from her refusal to believe that He was lost. "Then the disciples went away to their own homes": there was nothing more to be done; the grave was empty. They had examined the tomb and seen the napkin there; nothing was to be gained by aimless waiting. But Mary, though she knew what they had seen and had not a particle more of hope than they—Mary could not tear herself away but stood without at the sepulcher weeping. There is a kind of love that faces facts, and it is a noble and courageous love. It opens its eyes wide to dark realities, and bowing the head it says, "I must accept them." But there is an agony of love that does not act so; it hopes against hope and beats against all evidence. It is only women who can love like that, and it was a love like that which inspired Mary. No one will ever doubt John's love to Jesus. No one will ever doubt the love of Simon. "Simon, son of Jonas, lovest thou Me?" "Yea, Lord, Thou knowest that I love Thee." But the fact remains that on that Easter morning Peter and John went to their homes again, and only a woman lingered by the grave. I have not the least doubt that they urged her to go with them. They had been too long with Jesus not to be true gentlemen. It was cold and raw there, and the grass was wet, and it was dangerous for a woman with these Roman soldiers. But Mary simply replied, "I cannot go." She must linger and watch in the teeth of all the facts. And I say that measured by a test like that, there is not a disciple who can match the love of Mary.

---

2. From "To Homer" by John Keats (1795–1821), English poet.

The depth of Mary's love is also seen in her instant and glad obedience to her Lord. She would have flung herself upon His breast in her great joy, but Jesus said to her swiftly, "Touch Me not." You remember what Christ said when He appeared to Thomas? "Thomas, reach hither thy hand, and feel My wounds." To that disciple, torn with the stress of doubt, says the risen Savior, "Come and touch Me." But to Mary, whose doubts had all been scattered and who was filled with the wild joy of recognition, the Christ who said to Thomas, "Come and touch Me," said very swiftly and imperiously, "Touch Me not." What He meant was, "Things are all different now. You are to walk by faith and not by sight now. Do not think that My death is but a moment's break, and that the former life will be resumed. I ascend to the Father—old things have passed away—do not try to revive or recall these old relationships. Touch Me not, but go unto My brethren—tell them I am going home to God." That must have been a bitter disappointment to a heart so ardent and so intense as Mary's. The one thing she wanted was to be with Christ, yet that was the one thing which He denied her. And it is when I read how sweetly she obeyed, renouncing her own will to do Christ's bidding, it is then I realize how deep and true was the love of Mary for her Savior. There is a love that is loud in passionate protestations, but "methinks the lady doth protest too much."[3] Mary says little—does not protest at all—one word "Rabboni," and then her Master's bidding. And it is in that immediate obedience, which cut at the very root of all her joy, that he that hath eyes to see and ears to hear can gauge the height and depth of Mary's love.

In the last place, a word or two upon the revelation of the Lord to Mary. The unceasing wonder of it all is this, that to her *first* He should have showed Himself. Simon Peter had been at the tomb that morning, and "on this rock," said Jesus, "I will build My church." John had been at the sepulcher that morning—the disciple who had leaned upon Christ's bosom; yet neither to John nor to Peter had there been a whisper—no moving of pierced feet across the garden—all that was kept for a woman who had been a sinner and out of whom there had been cast seven devils. It is very notable that the first word of Christ after He had risen from the dead was *Woman*. "Woman, why weepest thou"—these are the first words which fell from the lips of Christ when He arose. And they tell us that though everything seemed different, yet there was one thing which death has failed to

3. From *Hamlet* by Shakespeare

alter, and that is the eyes of Christ for those who love Him and the sympathy of Christ for those who weep. You remember how, when Christ was in the wilderness, He was tempted to cast Himself down from the Temple. He was tempted to reveal Himself in startling fashion, as the Jews expected that Messiah would. But Christ resisted that spectacular temptation and showed Himself quietly to kindred hearts; and now after the grave has done its work, He is the very same Jesus as had His home in Nazareth. There are some arguments for the resurrection of the Lord which I confess do not appeal to me. They are too elaborate and metaphysical; they always leave some loophole of escape. But there is one argument that is irresistible and to me is overwhelming in its artless evidence, and that is the argument of this sweet incident. I could have believed the story was a myth if Christ had shown Himself upon the Temple steps. Had He appeared to Pilate and said, "Behold the Man," I could have believed it was an idle story. But that He should pass by Pilate and the people and His mother and John and James and Simon Peter, that He should show Himself first and foremost to a woman who had nothing to her credit but her love, I tell you that even the genius of a Shakespeare could never have conceived a scene like that. The strange thing is that what Christ did that morning, He has been constantly doing ever since. The first to see Him in all His power and love have been the very last the world expected. Do not pride yourself on your apostolate. There are things that you may miss for all your privileges. And some poor Magdalene, to whom you send the missionary, may be the first to hear the footfall on the grass.

And then Christ made Himself known by a single word. One word was enough when it was the woman's name. Jesus said unto her, "Mary," and she turned herself and said unto Him, "Rabboni." When Joseph made himself known unto his brethren, he stood in their midst and said to them, "I am Joseph." There are times when Jesus acts as Joseph did, and lifting up His voice cries, "I am Christ." But far more often when He reveals Himself, the first word that we hear is like this garden voice. It is not "I am Christ" that we first hear; the first word that we hear is "Thou art Mary." I mean by that that we are drawn to Christ by the deep and restful sense that we are known. Here is a Man who understands us thoroughly, who knows what we most need and what we crave for. And it is in response to that—which is the gospel call—that we turn our back on the grave, as Mary did, to find at our side One who has conquered death and who lives to be our Friend forevermore.

And it came to pass, after a while, that the
brook dried up (1 Kings 17:7).

11

The Failure of the Brook

W here this brook Cherith was, we do not know exactly. It was
one of the little tributaries of the Jordan. Somewhere in the uplands
of the south it had its rise, and it chattered as it flowed to join the
brimming river. It is notable that its name means "separated." It was
the lonely, separated burn.[1] There was that haunting sense of a deep
peace about it that we have felt beside some little stream among the
hills. For I know no place that is quite so full of God as a Highland
burn far in the Highland mountains, where the running water speaks
of unfailing life, and the hills of an eternity of calm. Here then, at
the beginning of his career, the prophet Elijah was sent apart by
God. Like Moses in Midian and like Jesus in the wilderness, God
drew him into isolation for a season. For very rarely does God
plunge His servants into the stir and dust of the great battle without
a call to a period of quietude when they can take their measure-
ments in silence.

Elijah, then, was sent to the brook Cherith by the express commandment of his God, and it must have been a strange and staggering thing for him when the waters of the brook began to fail. Had he
been fugitive from duty it would have been very different. He would

---

1. a brook or small stream

have taken that failure as his punishment. When we are false to duty, all the brooks dry up which once used to make music by our path. However dreary the road be, if a man is true to God the sound of water is never far away. It is when a man is false to God and duty that he walks continually by empty watercourses. But Elijah was not false to God or duty. It was the spirit of God that drove him out to Cherith. And God had said to him, "I shall feed thee there, and thou shalt drink of the brook and shalt be satisfied." Yet in spite of all that guidance and that promise in obedience to which Elijah had gone out—it came to pass after a while that the brook dried. Do you not think that was a staggering event? Can you not picture Elijah's incredulity? How he would disbelieve his senses and say, "It cannot be; this is some trick of my imagination." But at last the facts were too plain to be gainsaid—listen as he might there was no murmur— and every rock was hot in the strong sun, and the deep runnels of yesterday were empty. It was enough to crush an ordinary faith; but then the faith of Elijah was not ordinary. There is something noble in the man who in an hour like that can lift up his heart and say, "I trust in God." And I want to show you how that faith was justified and how there was deep meaning in that discipline, so that you and I may be a little stronger in those dark seasons when the brooks dry up.

First, then, the failure of the waters was meant to deepen the prophet's sense of brotherhood. He was drawn into a new fellow-ship with Israel in the very hour that Cherith ceased to flow. You must remember it was a time of drought. There had been no rain, and the whole land was parched. Little children were crying out for water, and mothers were peering into the depth of wells, and an-guished men were looking at the heavens and saying, "Pray God that it may rain today." Everywhere drought and cruel pangs of thirst and men and women entreating God for water—and all the time, in the little vale of Cherith, the coolness and the murmuring of the stream. It was very comfortable, and it was very happy, but it is not thus that Jehovah makes His prophets. What men have got to suffer they must suffer. What men have to endure they must endure. And so, that he might be a brother among brothers and feel his kinship with his suffering nation, it came to pass after a while that the brook dried.

Now I have little doubt that in a thousand lives that is still the secret of the failing brook. It is not because God is angry that it fails; it is because our Father wants us to be brothers. One touch of nature makes us all akin, even if it be only a touch of common thirst; and there is many a brook that the Almighty dries, so that we may cease from our pride and realize our kinship. There is no sympathy so deep and strong as that which springs out of a common suffering. Exclude a man from what others have to bear, and you exclude him from his heritage of brotherhood. But send him out into the boisterous world and let him bear your sorrow or your cross, and there is something in the very way he speaks to you that makes it evident he understands. Do you remember how the Pharisee prayed, "I thank Thee, God, I am not as other men"? The world was thirsty and crying out for water, and he was snug beside his running Cherith. It would have been better for him, in time and in eternity, had he been a little more like other men—and Elijah was saved from the Pharisaic temper by the unlooked-for drying of the brook. There are things, then, that it is hard to lose, but in God's sight it may be good to lose them. We grow more brotherly, more sympathetic, and more kind; life is fuller and richer and warmer than it once was. We were very superior and exclusive once, and the common people were odiously common—but it came to pass after a while that the brook dried.

Again Elijah was taught by this event that in certain matters God makes no exceptions. God has His chosen ones, but whatever they be chosen for, it is not to escape the heritage of tears. It is remarkable how little we know about Elijah. He steps as it were full-armed upon the stage. We know nothing of his childhood or his youth—nothing of his call to be a prophet. He is a prophet in the first glimpse we get of him, confronting Ahab in the name of God. Now to be a prophet was a lofty calling; it was to be in the counsels of Jehovah. By the very grandeur of his office there was a certain distance between the prophet and the ordinary man. And therefore it was reasonable to expect that the prophet would have a little special care and would be guarded, as the favorite of God, from some of the ills that flesh is heir to. I have no doubt that Elijah had such thoughts. I believe indeed that they never wholly left him. Long after this, it crushed him to the earth to think he was no better than his fathers. And God was teaching him how false it was to count on any exception as his right, when He dried up the waters of the Cherith. Elijah had to learn that though he was God's messenger, he was not going to escape the common lot. Called with a heavenly calling in Christ Jesus, he had to suffer some things like the vilest reprobate. He said, "I am a prophet, a chosen child of God; look how my brook is running when the rest are empty"—and it came to pass after a while that the brook dried.

Now that is a lesson we do well to learn; that in certain matters there are no exceptions. God has His chosen and peculiar people, but He never spares the rod to spoil His child. I had a visit from a friend the other day who was brokenhearted in unexpected grief. A little rivulet of life had made his meadow beautiful, when suddenly its music was no more. And "Oh," he said to me, "if I had been wicked—if I had been a rebel against God, I might have understood it; but it is hard to be dealt with thus when I have striven to serve Him and tried to be true to Him in home and business." You see at the heart of his so bitter grief there was a thought that is common to us all. My friend was like Elijah at his stream, saying, "I am a prophet and it can never dry." And one of the hardest lessons we must learn is that the name and nature of our God is love, yet for the man who trusts and serves Him best, there is to be no exception from the scourge. I think of Peter on whom the church is built, and when I open the door of his cottage there is fever there. I think of Mary, mother of our Lord, and what is that in her heart?—it is a sword. I think of the home at Bethany that Jesus loved—surely no blast of the chill wind will pierce that dwelling?—and it came to pass that their brother Lazarus died.

But I pass on, for I have one thing more to say, and it is the deepest lesson of the story. It is that the ceasing of the prophet's brook was the beginning of larger views of God. "Arise, get thee to Zarephath," said God; and Elijah arose and went down to Zarephath. Now there were two things that Elijah learned at Zarephath that were of mighty influence in his career. Zarephath was a heathen village given to the worship of Baal and reveling in the filth of that idolatry. And there, as Elijah viewed that superstition and realized the moral death which followed it, there was burned into his heart the loathing scorn that made him such an antagonist of Baal. But Elijah learned more at Zarephath than that. He learned there was a wideness in God's mercy. He saw that the God of Israel could be gracious to a woman who was born and bred a heathen. And to a Jew like Elijah, trained in the Jewish creed and believing that beyond the covenant was darkness, the thought that the mercy of God was for the heathen came with the thrilling of a great surprise. It was on that, you remember, that Jesus Christ laid stress, when He recalled this scene as He was preaching. "Were there no widows in

Israel," Jesus asked, "that Elijah must be sent to a poor heathen?"
And the Jews were so angry at that bare suggestion—at that scatter-
ing of covenant-mercy to the Gentile—that they shouted Him down
and dragged Him from the synagogue and would have murdered
the Messiah there and then. We are so familiar with the thought
now that to us it brings no gladness of surprise. But to Elijah—
fanatical Elijah—it came with the bitter-sweet of revelation. And
the prophet never would have been at Zarephath—never would
have been commanded to that place—had it not been for the failing
of the brook. There was something to learn so long as the brook
ran; there was something to learn also when it failed. There were
voices of God and of His worldwide mercy that were drowned by
the chatter and murmur of the stream. And so the stream was stilled,
and the brook dried, and Elijah had to take himself to heathendom,
there to see God and the largeness of His grace in a way that was
impossible at Cherith.

Now as it was with Elijah long ago, so I believe it often is today.
Let me suggest to you as I close two of our experiences on which
this discipline of the prophet may throw light.

Think first of the unquestioning trust of childhood, of the magnificent faith we had when we were young. "The poet is of imagination all compact," says Shakespeare, "but a little child is all
compact of faith."[2] I heard the other evening of two boys who were
playing at Elijah upon Carmel. And they built their altar out of
nursery chairs, and a little toy rabbit was their sacrifice. Then they
lay down upon the nursery floor, and they cried to God to send
down fire from heaven, and their mother told me how bitter was
their grief when they looked up, and the rabbit was untouched.
Well, you may smile at that, but to me it is super[3]—God is so near,
and heaven, and all the angels. There is a faith that runs through the
green fields of childhood, making everything it laps on fresh and
beautiful. Yet while some, it may be, never lose that faith, living in
its gladness until the end, for most of us it comes to pass that the
brook dries. There may be moral causes at the back of that. A vast
deal of doubt runs down to moral grounds. But if we are earnest and
truthful, and if we trust and pray, there is nothing to sigh for in the
failing brook. For the God whom we find again through many a
struggle, and the faith which we make ours by many a battle, and

---

2. From *A Midsummer Night's Dream* by Shakespeare
3. first rate, excellent

the things that we wrestle for until break of day, although we may go halting ever after—these are our own for time and for eternity, and neither life nor death can take them from us.

And then there are the blessings we enjoy—our health, our prosperity, the love of those who love us. There are many people who never lose these blessings, moving beside still waters to the end. But there are others with whom it is not so. They have suffered terribly or had sharp and sore reverses. There was a day when they had everything they wanted, but it came to pass after a while that the brook dried. I will not insult such by any platitudes. I will not give vacant chaff well meant for grain. I will only ask them, Has not God been nearer—has not religion been more to them since then? And if it has taken the failing of the stream to cast them utterly upon the arm of God, if they have risen from an empty brook to drink of an ocean that is ever full—perhaps it was not in anger but in love that the waters ceased to be musical at Cherith.

Death passed upon all men, for that all
have sinned (Rom. 5:12).

12

Sin and Death

There is perhaps no statement in all the writings of Paul that has
done more to discredit his authority than this one. That death, whenever it touches man, is the wages of sin; that had there been no sin
man would not have died is one of the sweeping statements of the
apostle that is rejected by many as ridiculous. That there are certain
sins which hand a man on to death is of course a fact which nobody
denies. There is not a doctor here but has seen people dying and
knew that they were dying because of their vicious lives. But Paul
is not talking here of vicious lives. He includes the child and the
saint and the purest and most tender woman, and he says of all of
them that but for sin there would have been no such experience as
death. It is that sweeping assertion which has been denied so vigor-
ously, and never more so than in the present day. That sin and death
should be so correlated is a statement that to many seems unwar-
ranted. And there are various ways, well known to students, in
which Christian thinkers have sought to meet the difficulty or to
evade the full significance of the words.

For instance there is one well-known theologian who insists that
all that the apostle means is this. All that he means is that the fact of
sin has given a peculiar character to death. Death might have been

very pleasant but for sin—a falling asleep under the kiss of God. But sin has come and made the struggle fearful and steeped the thought of death in gloom and horror; and it is that agony and dark foreboding, impressed by sin upon our dissolution, which the apostle is struggling to convey. Now no one denies that that is a great truth. The sting of death, Paul himself says, is sin. But if words are not an idle juggling, that is not what the apostle speaks of here. He is not talking of the accompaniments of death. He is talking here about the *fact* of death. He is not speaking of what makes death awful. He is speaking of death in itself—the naked fact. And if words mean anything, what Paul means here is this—*not* that sin has deepened the horrors of the grave, but that without sin there would have been no grave at all.

Again men have sought to evade these words by pushing death back, as it were, into another region. They say that what *we* call death is but a sleep, and that death is something far more terrible. Death is the separation of the soul from God. It is to be godless and loveless forever and forever. And it is of that eternal isolation, with its infinite and unutterable loneliness, that you must think when you read of sin and death. Once again I say all that is true— only it is not what Paul means here. Unless he means by death what the man in the street means when he loses his child or his sister or his friend, his argument is absolutely meaningless; and with all Paul's faults (and doubtless they are many) there is one I think he never has been charged with, and that is with losing his head in a great argument. You know what death is. Some of you have seen it. You have looked and cried brokenhearted, "He is dead." And it is of that—whether of saint or profligate—that the finger of God writes upon the wall—death passed upon all men, for that all have sinned.

Now I think there are two main reasons why men repudiate this, and the first has a peculiar weight today. It is the simple and incontestable fact that death was in the world long before man. No one denies that innumerable creatures were born and died long before man appeared. The story of geology has made that so plain that it is one of the commonplaces of our education. And if death was here long before sin was here—in other words the effect before the cause—does it not seem to invalidate the statement? If sin be the cause of death must not the order be, first, sin the cause, then, death as its effect? But as a matter of fact if there is one thing science has proved it is that the order is the reverse of that. And if death came first and sin long afterward—if a myriad creatures had died before man sinned—is it not absurd to say, as Paul says here, that death passed upon all men, for that all have sinned?

The other great objection to this statement is based on the universality of death. If man, and man alone, went to the grave, then death and sin might indeed be intertwined. But as man dies so does the sparrow die—so do the cattle upon a thousand hills—so does the beast that roams the untrodden forest, so does the thing that creeps under unfathomed seas. And beast and bird and monster in the deep—not one of them has ever known what sin is, yet they are in the grip of death no less than man. If sin and death be cause and effect, then wherever there is death there must be sin. Yet the sparrow cannot sin, nor can the worm, yet sparrow and worm no less than Shakespeare, die. And so we are told death is a natural thing. It is inherent in the very gift of life. And to couple sin and death as Paul has done is to perpetuate a Jewish superstition.

Now if this were a thought peculiar to St. Paul, we might be tempted just to leave it there. It is a kind of fashion to belittle St. Paul today, just as it is in literature to belittle Tennyson. But I think I could show you that so far from being Pauline, this is one pervading idea of the whole Testament. I think I could show you that it is a vital part of the message and of the method of the gospel. I think I could show you that in the thought of Jesus there is something monstrous and unnatural in death, and that it is not less certainly the child of sin because it is the sister of sweet sleep.

Take for example Christ at the grave of Lazarus. We read that He groaned in the spirit and was troubled there. These words are but feeble, compared with the original, to describe what was passing in the soul of Christ. A storm of passion swept across His spirit, and mingled with His pity there was indignation. Here was death's handiwork—here was death's triumph—and it stirred Christ to His depths to witness it. There was more than compassion in that storm-tossed soul; there was anger at the havoc of the grave. He was face to face with the mighty power of darkness, and it moved Him intensely and profoundly. I do not think that attitude of Jesus suggests that death was eminently natural. If it was natural and kindly, then to call Lazarus back was a most unnatural and unkindly thing. And so you see where Paul had learned his lesson—not in the dusty shelves of Jewish learning but by drinking deep of the spirit of the Master who had cried with a loud voice, "Lazarus, come forth."

Or think again of the agony in the garden—"If it be possible, let this cup pass from Me." And the sweat was as great drops of blood upon the ground, as the Savior was agonizing there. You say there is more than the fear of physical death in that—but I ask you, who gave you liberty to talk of physical death? When a friend dies, do you not say *he* is dead—do you not feel and know that *he* is *gone*? And death was terrible to Jesus Christ just because to Him it was far more than physical—it was the triumph of evil over the will of God, it was the very sacrament of sin. I say that you will never understand the agony unless for Christ, death was a monstrous thing. It was not the nails that He shrank from—not the pain; it was death—it was death itself, the fact of death. And probably that is why the fear of death has haunted some of the ripest saints the world has known. It is not that they were more cowardly than others. It is that, in Christ, death meant so much for them.

Or again, think of the words of Jesus as He sat at the last supper with His own. "This cup is the new testament in My blood, shed for many for the remission of sins." There is no question of what Jesus meant there. He is speaking of His death upon the cross. And the point I want you to note is how in the mind of Christ that death is linked with the pardon of our sin. Now if death and sin stand utterly apart, I do not hesitate to say these words of Christ are meaningless. If death and sin never touch—if they belong to different worlds—if sin is moral and if death is natural—I defy any man to establish correlation. Only if sin and death move on one level—only if they belong to the same sphere—is there the least hope of measuring sin by death or of finding in death the pardon of our sins. You cannot measure love, let me say, by heartbeats. The two belong to entirely different worlds. The one is a moral passion, the other a natural fact, and no man can intertwine or correlate them. And if death be natural and sin be moral, then to say Christ died for our sins is sheerest nonsense, and the gospel, which is founded upon that, crumbles at the touch of reason in the dust. I want you to feel, then, that the linking of sin and death is not just a rabbinical excrescence. I want you to feel that it runs like a thread of black through the whole tapestry of the evangel. And I want to tell you in closing why I think it possible, for one who joyfully accepts all facts of science, still to believe with all his heart that death passed upon all men because all have sinned.

In the first place, the Bible never doubts that death is natural to beast and bird. It does not say death passed upon all *beasts*; what it says is death passed upon all *men*. Now if man and beast were on a

similar footing—if man like the sparrow were but a part of nature—
then the argument from death's universality would be overwhelming, and you would rule out the very thought of sin. But the glory of
Christ is that He looks on man as something greater and grander
than a beast; so much more great, that what in the beast is natural,
in a God-enkindled humanity is monstrous. You say death is universal, therefore man must die; but do you not see that that *therefore* depends upon one thing? It depends on this, that in man there
are no elements, save the elements you discover in the beasts. If
there is more—if there is something higher—if there is that which
makes man kith and kin with God, then the introduction of that
higher factor makes death demand a different explanation. Now I
know that on one side of his being man is a part of nature; but on
another side he is the lord of nature. He can think long thoughts and
mold things to his will; he can lift up his eyes and cry, "There is a
God." And that moral and spiritual endowment of humanity sets
such a gulf between a man and nature, that to say because a beast
dies therefore man must die is hardly the logic that a Scotsman
loves. Some other explanation is demanded the moment you touch
the fringes of humanity. To measure a man by the measure of a
beast is to go back to a played-out materialism. And against *that* the
Bible sets its face, crowning man with glory and with honor, lifting
him up in dignity of life and setting him apart even in death.

Then, lastly, there are the thousand intimations that man is destined for an immortality. If death is natural, what do you make of
these? I had a friend who left for Canada the other day, and he took
some of his luggage into the cabin with him; but the great boxes
went down into the hold, and on each of them was written, "Not
wanted for the voyage." Every one of these chests was an absurdity
if all was over when the ship reached Halifax—and man has a
hundred things "Not wanted for the voyage"—things that are meaningless without a life beyond. Now remember that the New Testament knows nothing of a shadowy immortality of souls. It is *man*
that is immortal, soul and body, each glorified to be the organ of the
other. And if in the progress toward that immortality there comes a
moment when these twain are sundered—a moment when soul and
body, which make man, are torn apart by a relentless power—I say
that that calls for an explanation which the death of bird or beast
does not demand. Are you able to offer any explanation? Do you
know of any answer to that problem? The answer of the Word of
God is this, "Death passed upon all men, for that all have sinned."

The destruction that wasteth at noonday
(Ps. 91:6).

13

The Perils of the Middle-Aged

In every literature the life of man is pictured under the symbol of a day. There is something in the rise and setting of the sun that answers so closely to life's start and close that the correspondence has been universally perceived. We speak of the morn of infancy or childhood; we describe old age as the evening of our day; declining years are the afternoon of life; and final efforts the lingering gleams at sunset. It is in such language, drawn from the sphere of day, that we imaginatively describe the facts of life. This being so, you will at once perceive the meaning we may attach to noonday. The noonday of life is the time of middle age, when the morning freshness of youth has passed away. And so the destruction which wastes at the noonday, whatever be its literal significance, may without any violence be referred to the peculiar temptations of that period. That, then, is the theme which I would speak upon—the perils that beset the middle-aged. I shall not speak directly to the young, nor shall I offer counsel to the old. But I shall address myself more immediately to those who are in the noontide of their days—in the long stretch that we call middle life.

I do so with all the greater readiness because this is a period so often overlooked. For a hundred special sermons to young men, you will scarce find one which appeals to middle age. No doubt there is something to be said for that, for youth is the time of impression and resolve, and the preacher feels that if he can influence youth, the trend of the later period is determined. But along with this wise reason goes another, which is as unwise as it is false, and which is specially cogent with young ministers. It is the thought that after the storms of youth, middle age is as a quiet haven. It is the thought that youth is very perilous, and middle age comparatively safe. It is the thought that as a man enters manhood he is encompassed by quicksands and hidden rocks and shoals uncharted, but that in middle age all these are past, and the barque[1] has entered quiet and restful waters. I think that nothing could be more untrue than that. I think no outlook could be more pernicious. I am convinced that of all moral perils none are more deadly than the perils of the noonday. And could we but read the story of this city and of the lives in it that in the sight of God have failed, I believe we should find that the sins of middle age have been more disastrous than the sins of youth. On that, then, let me speak a little—on the temptations peculiar to this period. And so may God, who has spared us through our youth, safeguard us from the destruction that wastes at noonday.

Now one of the great features of middle age is this—and of course I can only speak in general terms—one of the features of middle age is this, that by that time a man has found his lifework. No longer does he look forth with dim surmise, wondering what may be the burden of the future. No longer does he turn to every hand, in doubt as to the path he must pursue. But whether by choice, or by necessity, or by what men might call an accident, he has taken up once and for all his calling and settled down to the business of his life. When one stands amid the Alps in early morning it is often impossible to tell mountain peak from cloud. For the rising sun, touching the clouds with glory, so fashions them into fantastic pinnacles that it would take a practiced eye to tell which is cloud and which is snow-capped summit. But when noonday comes there is no longer difficulty. The clouds have separated and have disappeared, and clear and bold into the azure sky there rises up the summit of the Alp. So in our morning hour it is often hard to tell which is the cloud-capped tower and which the hill. But as the day advances and the sun mounts to noonday, that problem of the morning disappears. For clear above us rises the one summit—clear before us stretches the one work. For weal

---

1. boat or sailing vessel

or woe we have now found our lifework, nor are we likely to change it until the end.

Now with this settlement into a single task there generally comes a certain happiness. We are freed from many disquieting uncertainties that vexed us when we stood upon life's threshold. Unless a man's work be utterly abhorrent—so uncongenial as to be abhorrent—there is a quiet pleasure in those very limits that are the noticeable marks of middle age. The river no longer frets among the rocks nor is there any glory now of dashing waterfall, but in the tranquil reaches there is a placid beauty and the suggestion of abiding peace. Nay more, there is an ingathering of strength—the strength that always comes of concentration. No longer does a man dissipate his powers in trying to open doors that have been barred. But knowing his work and knowing his limitations, he gives himself with his whole heart to the one thing, and so is a stronger man in middle age than he was in the happy liberty of youth.

But just here arises one danger of that period—one form of the destruction that wastes at noonday—and it lies in the contraction of the manhood to the one groove in which the lifework runs. The eager expectancy of youth is gone. The range of opening manhood is no more. Absorbed in the business on which his living hangs, a man contracts into a businessman. There was a day when he felt the charm of nature, but the voices of nature mean little to him now. There was a day when poetry could move him, but it is many years since he has read a poet. Strong because concentrated in his life's great work, he may be weak in that very concentration. Quietly happy because he has found his groove, he may be further from God than in his wayward youth. There is a form of question which we often use. We ask of such and such a man, "What is he?" And you know the answer which we expect to get—he is a "teacher, a doctor, or an engineer." Now if the end for which a man was born was to be a doctor or an engineer, happy indeed would be that noonday. But when we remember what man is and yet shall be, when we pass in review the powers of his prime, when we think of Him in whose image man is made (which image it is the lifework to restore), do we not feel what an irony it is, and what a condemnation of the noonday, that we should say of a man he *is* a draughtsman, or of another, he *is* an engineer? Has the promise of the morning come to this? Are these the feet that are set in a large room?[2] Has all the love

---

2. Psalm 31:8

that blessed the years of childhood, all the preventing mercies of the spirit, all the romance and poetry of youth, all the thoughts that wandered through entirety—have all these been lavished on a man that he might become a first-rate man of business? No matter how successful a man be, if he is impoverished and contracted by success, then in the sight of God he is in peril of the destruction that wastes at noonday.

Faced, then, by that peril as we are, how may we reasonably hope to overcome it? One way is to have some lively interest out of the single line of the career. It may be books, it may be pictures, or it may be flowers; it may be politics, it may be music. It does not really matter what it is, if it be an avenue into a larger world. I never knew a man who had a hobby, even if it were collecting beetles, but it tended to keep him from being a mere machine and helped him through the perils of the noonday. But there is something better than a hobby. It is the symmetry of the character of Jesus. It is the thought that there once moved on earth a Man who was perfect in the whole range of manhood. That is the value of fellowship with Christ in an age when specialism is inevitable. That is the value of fellowship with Christ in a city where men are bound to concentrate. Christ touches every string upon the harp. He vitalizes powers we would ignore. He came to give life and to give it more abundantly, and so He saves from the destruction of the noonday.

Once more, one of the perils of the noonday is the decay and the deadening of faith. There is no period in the whole course of life in which it is so hard to walk by faith. In childhood, faith is an abiding habit. A child has a perfect genius for trusting. Dependent for everything upon the care of others, to lean on others is a sheer necessity. And so in youth is found the trustful habit, that happy reliance upon another's love, which makes the child, no matter what his faults, the type of the citizen in Jesus' kingdom. Then in old age and when the sun is westering, faith surely must become easier again. Standing so near the margin of this world, has a man no gleams and visions of the next? So soon to make that plunge into the darkness and to leave forever the "old familiar faces," how utterly and hopelessly hardened must he be who has no thought save for the things he sees! I do not say that faith is ever easy. It is the greatest of ventures and of victories. It is the victory that overcomes the world and not to be won without a weary battle. But I do say that in youth with its dependence and in age when the ship is so near the boundless deep, there is not a little to wean the heart from faithlessness, not a little that is provocative of trust.

But in middle age, as you will see at once, these helps and encouragements are wholly wanting. There is neither the stimulus of youth nor of age to lead a man to trust in the unseen. No more are we dependent upon others as we were in the happy and careless days of childhood. No more do we lean upon a father's love for the food we eat and for the clothes we wear. We are self-dependent now, and self-reliant; it is by the toil of our own hand we live. Once we depended upon another's labor, but now our livelihood hangs upon our own. Then, too, in the time of middle age there is generally a reasonable measure of good health. The days succeed each other at an even pace, and before us lies an unbroken stretch of road. Not yet do we discern the shades of evening nor feel on our cheek the chill wind of the twilight. We are far away from the brink of the beyond.

It is such facts as these that hint to us of the destruction that wastes at noonday. No period is so prone to materialize the spirit or to blind a man to the range of the unseen. Then first relying on our personal effort and through our effort achieving some success, then first awakening to the power of money and to all that money is able to procure, still unvisited by signs of dissolution and reasonably secure of many years, it is in middle age we run the tremendous peril of becoming worldly and materialized. Youth has its dangers, but they are those of passion, and in all passion there is something great. Very disastrous are the sins of youth, yet is there a noble lavishness about them. But the sins of middle age, though not so patent, yet in the sight of God may be more deadly, for they lead to that encrustation of the spirit which the Bible calls the hardening of the heart. You get a company of middle-aged men together and listen to their talk about their neighbors. Is it not certain to come round to money, to their losses and to their successes and their incomes? I do not imply that what they say is scandal. I do not even suggest it is uncharitable. I only say that they have materialized since the happy days when they were boys together. There is no time when it is harder to walk with God than on the levels of our middle age; none when it is more difficult to keep alive the vision of the eternal and unseen. For the sweet dependence of childhood is no more, and the heart has awaked to the power of the material, and not yet does the hand of death knock loudly. Brethren, who like myself have entered these mid-years, remember that Christ is praying that your faith fail not. He knows the arrow that flies in the morning; He knows the destruction that wastes at noonday. From the hard and worldly heart may Christ deliver us. May He give us the hope that is cast within the veil. Not slothful in business but toiling at it heartily, may we endure as seeing Him who is invisible.

But not only is middle age the time when we are in peril of losing faith in God. It is also very notably the time when we are in danger of losing faith in man. The two things indeed may be said to go together, the one making way for and drawing on the other, for between faith in man and faith in God, there is ever the most vital of connections. In our days of childhood we believe in men with a romantical and splendid trust. We have not yet come into contact with them nor learned the common motives that inspire them. It is from our father we take our ideas of manhood; it is from our mother we take our ideas of womanhood; and the father is ever a hero to the child, and the mother is ever worthy to be loved. Then we begin to read, and in our books we find the story of great and noble actions; nor do we think of these as something rare, on the contrary we father them on every man we meet, so that all history in childish eyes is little else than a book of golden deeds. And then again, as the poet Wordsworth[3] taught us, we clothe man in the charm of his surroundings, giving to every shepherd on the hills something of the strength of the hills on which he moves, and thinking that the life of the cottage must be beautiful, because it nestles in a scene of beauty. So do we stand on the threshold of maturity, never yet brought into close touch with men, and believing in manhood with a perfect trust, yet with a trust which never has been tried.

And then with middle age comes the awaking. We see how different men are from our dreams. The vision we had of them is rudely shattered, and with the shattering there goes our faith. It may be that a young man goes to business under an employer who is a professing Christian. He may even be a pillar in the church in which the young man was baptized and trained. But in the business there are such shady tricks, such practices incompatible with honor, that in a year or two not all a father's pleading can prevail with his son to take the holy sacrament. It may be that a woman is deceived in love by some one of whom once she thought the world. It may be that a daughter lives to see that the mother whom she adored is but a worldly woman. Or it may be that, without sudden shock, we

---

3. William Wordsworth (1770–1850), English poet, poet laureate 1843–1850.

slowly discover the wheels within the wheels, the rottenness in much that is called business, the worship of money in much that is called the church, and the mean hunting after place and power that flaunts itself as patriotic politics. Every man who is the least in earnest has to pass through that disenchantment in some form. Very commonly it meets a man as youth expires and middle age begins. And it is this passage from the hopes of youth to the chilling experience of middle life that is so often attended by an eclipse of faith. Some men it makes utterly hardhearted; others, it makes tolerantly cynical. To some it is a positive relief to find the world no better than themselves. But to all it is a deadly peril, far more insidious than sins of youth—it is the destruction that wastes at noonday.

There is but one help in that temptation—one help, yet it is all-sufficient. It is to remember that though He knew the worst, Christ never for an hour lost faith in man. Despised, deceived, rejected, and betrayed, still in the eyes of Christ was manhood noble. His own forsook Him on the way to Calvary, and yet He loved His own unto the end. Great is our need of Christ in time of youth if we are to steer our barque amid its shoals. Great is our need of Christ when we are old if we hope to enter the eternal city. But not less great is our need of Jesus Christ in the dusty levels of our middle age if we are to be saved from that destroying angel—the destruction that wastes at noonday

I Daniel alone saw the vision: for the
men that were with me saw not the vision
(Dan. 10:7).

14

The Unseen Vision

Cyrus had been king of Babylon three years when this revelation
was vouchsafed to Daniel. In the first month, on the four-and-
twentieth day of it, he had a vision of the eternal Son. He was
walking and meditating by the river Hiddekel when there broke
mysteriously on his gaze a Man, and this Man, as seen again in the
Apocalypse, we know to have been the preexistent Christ. He was
clothed with linen as a priest is clothed. He was girded with gold as
one on royal service. His body was as a beryl, and his eyes like fire,
and the voice of His words like the voice of a multitude. And so
overpowering in its glory was it all, so suddenly and so divinely
splendid, that the comeliness of Daniel was turned into corruption,
and he retained no strength. No wonder that Daniel was profoundly
astonished that no one had seen the vision but himself. "I Daniel
alone saw the vision, for the men who were with me saw it not."

That circumstance at once suggests to me that vision is not con-
ditioned by locality. Daniel and his friends were all in company by
the banks of the river Hiddekel that evening. There was the river,
broad, still, magnificent. There were the plains and far away the
hills. And the birds cried, and the reeds by the water whispered, and

faintly from a distance came the stir of Babylon. It was the same murmur that fell on every ear. It was the same scene that opened on every eye. Now if what a man saw depended on environment, there would have been no one blind by Hiddekel that night. On every eye of that little strolling company would have flashed the shining vision of the Christ. But "I Daniel alone saw the vision, for the men that were with me saw it not."

The same thing meets us in life on every hand, meets us, for instance, in the case of poets. Set down a poet on any spot on earth, no matter how bleak and barren be the place, and he will enmantle it with gold and glory and have his vision in it of all lovely things. David Gray[1] spends his childhood by the Luggie,[2] and the Luggie makes music for him like any fount on Helicon.[3] Tannahill[4] goes out in the evening to Gleniffer Braes,[5] and they kindle his heart into the flame of song. The Ettrick Shepherd[6] moves on the lonely hills, but in every glen is the flash of mystic figures. And Robert Burns has thoughts too deep for tears as he lovingly haunts the windings of the Doon.[7] Were these men alone as they walked by their river Hiddekel? Were there no other shepherds in Ettrick than James Hogg? Ah, it is not the place that makes the difference; it is the heart that beats upon the place. I Daniel, I Burns, I Tannahill—I, walking through this wonderful world—*I* saw the vision, but the men who were beside me saw it not.

The same thing, again, is very true of pioneers in social reform. All their achievement runs right back to this, that they alone had the vision by the river. I can picture the first poor homeless waif who arrested the gaze of a Dr. Barnardo.[8] Many an eye had glanced at him that night; and some had bidden him move on, and some had

---

1. I have designedly chosen illustrations which would appeal to a West of Scotland audience; but I cannot help thinking that David Gray has not yet come to his own. In *The Luggie and Other Poems* there is poetry of the finest kind. On Gray's short and sad life, see *David Gray and Other Essays* by Robert Buchanan, and *Buchanan's Life* by Harriet Jay.

2. The Scottish river Luggie

3. Helicon—mountain in south central Greece, the abode of Apollo and the Muses.

4. Robert Tannahill (1774–1810), Scottish songwriter.

5. the hill district

6. "The Ettrich Shepherd" by James Hogg (1770–1835), Scottish poet.

7. The Scottish river Doon

8. Thomas John Barnardo (1845–1905), English physician, social reformer, and philanthropist.

pitied him; but "I Daniel alone saw the vision," and it was the vision that made all the difference. A vision of that boy clothed and redeemed, engirdled by the ministries of love; a vision of the boy out on the fields of Canada with the wind of the hills and the sunshine on his cheek. And thousands passed the waif, hurrying along, bent on the business or revelry of Babylon; but the men that were with him did not see the vision. We talk with a certain contempt about the visionary, and the man who is *merely* a visionary is contemptible. But all great movements for bettering mankind have begun not in a brain that schemed but in a heart that saw. And it is because the others by the river see everything save the vision of the Daniel, that social toilers have been laughed to scorn, until some of them have been brokenhearted.

The same thought also serves to illuminate much of the heroism that men display in suffering. How we conduct ourselves in days of strain very largely depends on what we see. I heard the other day of an old man who was dying of an excruciating trouble. And his minister, doing his poor best to comfort him, said, "Courage, friend, you will soon be in heaven." "Why, sir," said the old saint, "what do you mean? I've been in heaven for twenty years." *That* was the secret of the heroic courage that amazed the world in the early Christian martyrs. That was why tender women and fond mothers could sacrifice everything they loved for Christ. It was not that they were stronger than the heathen; but it was that they saw more than the heathen—they saw through the veil into another kingdom, where Christ was enthroned at the right hand of God. I stood a few months ago in one of those amphitheaters[9] where the Christian martyrs used to be put to death. It was a little worn by the storms of countless years, but so perfect that bull-fights are still held in it. And as I pictured the thousands who once filled these seats and gazed on the battle with the wild beasts below, I thought how perfectly they could see everything, except the one thing that made all the difference. The crowds that were gathered there saw not the vision. They saw not the Man girt with the golden girdle. And so they were amazed that some poor slave should put their philosophers to shame in fortitude.

This, too, is preeminently true of Christ. It helps us better to comprehend His loneliness. If He was separated from His race by being sinless, He was separated not less by what He saw. Jesus

9. Nimes, France

often complained that men were *blind*—as if in that there lay all manner of evil; and how blind they must have seemed to Him we may conjecture when we remember that He saw a kingdom in a mustard seed. One day when He was seated at a meal there entered a woman who began to anoint His feet; and the men who were seated with Him said, "If He but knew—if He only knew that creature as we do!" But Christ did more than know, Christ had a vision of her, pardoned, restored, rebeckoned[10] to her womanhood; and the men who were with Him at the feast saw not the vision. We talk of seeing eye to eye with anybody; but no one ever saw eye to eye with Christ. He saw such heights and depths and undiscovered glories that, matched with His, the keenest eyes are blind. There is a deep sense in which that kingly vision has proved the regeneration of the world.

But there is another suggestion in the words; it is that the secret of vision lies in character. Why, think you, did these men who were with Daniel see nothing of the glory in the heavens? I shall advance two reasons for it, and so close.

In the first place, they were not on the path of duty. They had no business to be loitering by the Hiddekel. They should have been home in Jerusalem with the exiles who had returned and who now were busy rebuilding the ruined city. What right had they to be lingering in Babylon? Why had they not crossed the desert with their countrymen? It was such a smooth and easy life in Babylon that they shirked the toil and the hardship of return. Daniel was there because God willed it so. The work of Daniel was by the side of Cyrus. And therefore Daniel had his vision there, because he was in his God-appointed place. But those who were with him did not see the vision—no glory of Christ surprised them by the river— because they had chosen the life of selfish ease in preference to the rougher path of duty.

What that means is that if we are false to duty, we may be certain we shall never see the best. My finest holiday, Mohammed used to say, is the day on which I do my duty. Do you think that life is ever royal to the pleasure-seeker? Do you think that our smart society is really to be envied? The commonest day has something to reveal which it never shows save to the dutiful. "I am come to do Thy will, O God," said Christ, and that was the secret of His amazing vision. In every flower and in every heart there was a depth of meaning for

---

10. summoned again

Him because He was obedient. And so with us, if instead of seeking pleasures we seek to be quietly faithful in our place; if we will scorn delights and live laborious days, struggling to be true rather than to be happy; then all unexpectedly the clouds will break sometimes, and we shall hear strains of music unforgettable, and so shall we be stronger for the warfare, as knowing that we are not far from God.

Then, in the second place, they did not see the vision because they felt not the burden and sorrows of Israel. That burden had well-nigh broken Daniel's heart, but there is no sign that it troubled them at all. For three weeks Daniel had mourned and fasted. For three weeks he had been praying for his people. In all their affliction Daniel was afflicted, crying to God for his unhappy countrymen. But the men who were with him had no such intense sympathy; there is not a trace that their hearts were torn for Israel; and so when the Lord of Israel appeared to Daniel, the men who were with him did not see the vision. Must there not always be a preparation of that kind if we are to see the vision of Christ Jesus? It is when we feel the weight and guilt of sin that we realize our need of a Redeemer. The man who has seen the depths of his own heart and known how tangled are the roots of evil is ready for the appearing of the Lord, clad in the garments of His priestly office. That is one spiritual gain of passing years; they show us more plainly our utter need of Christ. Someone to die for us—someone to bear our guilt—I think we all come back to that at last. May each of us have that saving vision now and again by the river to which we all are hastening—a river where on this side is farewell, and on the other the welcome of the morn.

My meat is to do the will of Him that sent
Me (John 4:34).

15

The Dedication of the Will

It has been a matter of controversy time and time again which is
the true well-spring of religion; and to this question, which is fresh
in every age, there are two answers which demand attention.

On the one hand there are many reverent thinkers who trace the
roots of religion to the reason. It is because we are reasonable
beings that we know the infinite reason, which is God. A dumb
beast is not endowed with reason, though the rudiments of it be
latent in its instinct. It is man alone, lifting his forehead heavenward, who is a truly reasonable creature; and in man alone, because
he is so gifted, is there the craving for the eternal being and the
assurance, at the back of all things visible, of a hand that guides and
of a heart that plans. Thought is the lattice through which the human spirit peers forth upon the vista of eternity. Thought is the
mystical ladder that goes heavenward and lifts itself through the
silence to the throne. And if the angels, clad in their garb of ministry, move up and down upon its steps of radiance, it is because the
head that lies upon the pillow is that of a reasonable man.

On the other hand there have been many thinkers who have
denied this primary place to thought. It is not from reason that
religion springs, they tell us; it is from the deeper region of the

feelings. How can the fragmentary thought of man reach forth to the perfect thought of the Almighty? Can any by intellectual searching find Him out, and are not His thoughts different from our thoughts? Do we not know, too, that an age of so-called reason is never a time when eternal things are clear, but always a time when voices are but faint that come with the music of the faraway? On these grounds there has been raised a protest against reason as the wellspring of religion. Not upon reason is religion based; it sinks its shaft into the depth of feeling. It is born in the longing you cannot analyze, in the emotion that is prior to all thought, in the craving for God that rests upon no proof and stirs in a depth below the reach of argument.

But when we turn to the word of Jesus Christ and to its translation in apostolic doctrine, we discover that neither thought nor feeling is laid at the foundation of religion. Christ had no quarrel with the human intellect. He recognized its wonder and its power. His own intellectual life was far too rich for Him to be a traitor to the brain. Nor was Christ the enemy of human feeling. He never made light of most tender emotion. He who wept beside the grave of Lazarus could never be the antagonist of tears. But in the teaching of Christ it is not thought nor feeling that is the well-spring of personal religion. "My meat is to do the will of Him that sent Me"; the well-spring is in the region of the will. It is *there* that a man must pass from death to life. It is *there* that the path of piety begins—not in the loftiest and holiest thought nor in the rapture of excited feeling. The first thing is the dedication of the will, the response of a free man to a great God, the yielding of self to that imperious claim which is made by the loving Father in the heavens. "Seek ye first the kingdom of God and His righteousness"—"Let the dead bury their dead, follow thou Me"—such are the words in which our Lord describes the primary and determinative action. A man may cherish the most reverent thought or may luxuriate in most tender feeling, yet if he harbor an unsurrendered will, he knows not yet the meaning of religion.

It is thus that we begin to understand the condemnation of Christ on indecision. "He that is not with me, is against Me"—"No man can serve two masters." No matter how ignorant a man might be, Christ never was without hope for him. No matter how depraved he was, there was a spark within him that might be fanned to flame. But of all men the most hopeless in Christ's sight was the irresolute and undecided person; the man who refused to take a spiritual stand

and who was contented aimlessly to drift. It is very probable that Judas Iscariot was a man of such irresolution. It had been growing increasingly clear to him, as months went by, that he was hopelessly out of sympathy with Jesus. But instead of arising in some great decision that might have closed that mockery of following, he drifted, amid ever quickening waters, until suddenly—the whirlpool and the cry. The man who hesitates, we say, is lost—but Christ has come to seek and save the lost. Am I speaking to any waverer tonight, to any hesitating, undecided person? My brother, until the will is right, nothing is right. No man is Christ's until the will has yielded.

> Our wills are ours, we know not how;
> Our wills are ours to make them Thine.

It is further notable in this connection that Jesus never overpowered the will. It was His glory to *empower* it, but to *overpower* it He scorned. "Come unto Me, and I will give you rest"—a man must come; no hand from heaven will drag him. No irresistible and irrational constraint will force him into the presence of the Savior. A man is something better than a beast—he is but a little lower than the angels—and as a man, or not at all, Christ will have the allegiance of the will. "Ye will not come to Me that ye might have life"—there is the ring of an infinite pity about that; but the other side of that so baffled yearning reveals the very grandeur of humanity. For it tells of a being whose heritage is freedom—not to be overborne by God Himself—of one who must come with a freely yielded will or else not come at all. With Mohammed it was the Koran or the sword, and that compulsion was a degradation. Hence never, under Mohammedan dominion, has manhood risen to its highest splendor. But with Christ there was no compulsion of the will, save the compulsion of overmastering love, and that great recognition of our freedom has blossomed into the flower of Christian manhood. Do not wait, then, I would beg of you, as if a day were coming when you *must* be good. Do not think that the hour will ever strike when you will be swept irresistibly into the kingdom. At the last it is a matter of decision; and in all the changes of the coming years, never will it be easier for you to make the great decision than tonight.

We might further illustrate Christ's emphasis on will by some of the relationships in which He sets it. Think first of its relationship to action. It is not the action in itself that Jesus looks at; He has a gaze that pierces deeper than the action. He sees at the back of every deed its motive, and that is the measure of value in His sight. Viewed from the standpoint of the day's collection there was no great value in the widow's mite. One coin out of the pocket of the rich was worth a hundred such in some eyes. But there is a certain kind of calculation that is intolerant of all arithmetic, and it was always on that basis Christ computed. Was there no sacrifice behind that little gift which was dropped so quietly into the temple treasury? Was there no will so bent upon obedience that it must pour its all into the offering? What Jesus saw was not the sorry mite; it was the dedicated will behind the mite. An action had no value in Christ's eyes unless at the back of it there was the willing mind. Deep down, in the unseen springs of a man's being, lay that which determined the value of his conduct. And that is the reason why Christ appraises action in a way that so often seems inexplicable and is sublimely careless of the common standards by which the world distributes its applause.

Or think of the relationship of will to knowledge if you want to know how Christ regarded will. "If any man willeth to do His will, he shall know of the doctrine whether it be of God." If any man willeth to do His will—then at the back of true knowledge is obedience, and what we know of the highest and the best ultimately depends upon the will. Let a man refuse to submit his will to God, and the gateway of truth is closed to him forever. No daring of intellect will pierce its deeps, nor will any imagination see its beauty. Truth at the heart of it is always ethical, kindred in being to man's moral nature; and if that nature be choiceless and disordered, the power and majesty of truth are never known. That is the reason why the simplest duty has always an illuminative power. Do the next thing, and do it heartily, and the very brain will grow a little clearer. For the word of God is a lamp unto our feet, and only when our feet go forward bravely will the circle of light advance upon the dark and reveal what is always shadowed to the stationary. It is not merely by His depth of thought that Christ has kindled the best thought of Christendom. It is by his urgent and passionate insistence upon the dedication of the will. And men have obeyed Him and taken up their cross and followed bravely when all in front was shrouded, to find that they were moving into a larger world and under the archway of a brighter heaven.

Or think of the relationship of will to fellowship—man's spiritual fellowship with his Redeemer. That friendship is not based on fellow-feeling; it is based, according to Christ, on fellow-will. "Behold, Thy mother and Thy brethren seek Thee"; and Jesus answered, "Who, then, is My brother? He that doeth the will of My Father in heaven, the same is My mother, My brother, and My sister." It is not a question, then, of what you know, if you are to be a brother or sister of the Lord. It is not a matter of excited feeling nor of any glowing or ecstatic rapture. He that does the will—though it be often sore, and though the way be dark, and though the wind be chill—he that does the will of My Father which is in heaven, the same is My sister and My brother. That means that on dedication of the will depends all fellowship with Jesus Christ. We must say, "Take my will, and make it Thine," if we are to be numbered of His company. And if fellowship with Him be true religion—the truest and purest the world has ever known—you see how it does not rest on thought or feeling but has its well-spring in the surrendered will.

And in the life of Christ this is the crowning glory—a will in perfect conformity with God's. He is our Savior and our great example because of that unfailing dedication. Look at Him as He is tempted in the wilderness—is there not there a terrible reality of choice? Does there not rise before Him the alternative of self, to be instantly and magnificently spurned? And ever through the progress of His years, His meat is to do the will of God who sent Him; until at last, upon the cross of Calvary, the dedication is perfected and crowned. I want you then ever to remember that the will is the very citadel of manhood. To be a Christian that must be yielded up. Everything else without it is in vain. Religion founded on feeling is unstable. A religion of intellect is cold and hard. Total surrender is what Christ demands, and in it lies the secret of all peace.

Consider the lilies of the field (Matt. 6:28).

16

A Sermon for Springtime

At this sweet and hopeful season of the year,[1] when the freshness and beauty of the spring surround us, I am sure there are few
of us whose thoughts do not go forth to the wonder and the glory of
the world. After the deadness of our northern February, springtime
comes tingling with the surprise of joy, and that is indeed one of our
compensations for the stern and desolate winter of our land. Of all
our poets who "build the lofty rhyme,"[2] there is none more thoroughly English than the poet Chaucer.[3] As we read his musical and
vivid verse, it is always the sound of a brother's voice we hear. And
in nothing is he more truly English than in this, that he stirs at the
call of the sweet voice of April and, casting his books aside, longs
to become a child of his warm and beautiful and gladsome world.
In some measure all of us feel that; nor is there aught unworthy in
that restlessness. Rightly used, it may be a means of grace, drawing
us nearer to the feet of Christ. And therefore I like at this season of
the year to speak sometimes on the ministry of nature and to discover what that meant for Jesus.

Now in this matter there is one thing which strikes me, and that

1. Preached in the month of April.
2. From "Lycidas" by Milton.
3. Geoffrey Chaucer (1340?–1400), English poet.

is the contrast between Christ and Paul. You never feel that Paul is at home in the country. You always feel that Paul is at home in the city. Country life did not appeal to Paul; it did not flash into spiritual suggestion as he viewed it. He heard the groans of a travailing creation, but he did not love it to its minutest feature. It was the city which appealed to Paul, with its great and crying problems of humanity, with its pageantry and its murmuring and its stir, with its crowds that would gather when one began to preach. The kingdom of heaven is not like a seed to Paul; the kingdom of heaven is like some noble building. When he would illustrate the things of grace, he does not turn to the vine or the lily. He turns to the soldier polishing his armor, to the gladiator fighting before ten thousand eyes, to the freeborn citizen whose civic charter had been won in the senate of imperial Rome. I need hardly wait to indicate to you how different this is from Christ's procedure. Not in the city did Jesus find His parables, save when He saw the children in the marketplace. He found them in the clustering of the vine. He found them in the springing of the corn. He found them in the lake where boats were rocking and in the glow of sunset and of sunrise. He found them in the birds that wheeled above Him—in the fig tree—in the fowl of the farmyard. He found them in the lily of the field, with which even Solomon could not compare.

It is for that reason that when the springtime comes I always thank God that Christ was bred at Nazareth. We owe far more to that quiet home at Nazareth than some of us may be ready to acknowledge. Paul was a native of Tarsus—no mean city. It was a place like Glasgow, the seat of a wide commerce. Paul was a city boy, bred among city streets, familiar with crowds since he had eyes to see. And though the gardens of a Roman city were very beautiful in their arrangement, yet gardens and fountains are a sorry substitute for the lone glen and the silence of the hills. But in the providence of God, Christ was a country child. There was no "Please keep off the grass" at Nazareth. Trespassers were never prosecuted on the hills there, as they ought never to be in any country. And it was there that Jesus spent His boyhood—keen-eyed, quick-hearted, loving all God's creatures, moving, as if at home, where all was beautiful, and praying best because He loved it all. That is the note which you detect at once when you come to the public ministry of Jesus. Other teachers elaborate their parables; but with Christ they come welling up out of the heart. They were His heritage from the

quiet days of Nazareth when He had watched and loved and understood. It was His manhood recalling in the strife the music that had
charmed Him as a child.

Again, if Christ is different from Paul in this matter, He is equally
distinguished from His Jewish ancestry. The fact is that in His
attitude toward nature you can never historically account for Jesus. I
believe that sometimes we misrepresent the Jews here. We contrast
them too dogmatically with the Greeks. We think of the Jews as so
intensely spiritual that they were blind to the beauty of the world.
But no one who has studied his Old Testament dare make a sharp
distinction such as that, for the Old Testament that is afire with God
is redolent from first to last of nature. The truth is that Jew no less
than Greek looked with the most intense interest on nature. Both
felt the abiding magic of its power; both bowed before its ever-
changing mystery. But to the Greek the world was just the world,
gladsome and fair, a thing to be desired; while to the Jew the world
was always wonderful, because it was instinct and aflame with
God. Into that heritage Jesus Christ was born. Remember He was a
Jew after the flesh. Yet when we read His teaching about nature, we
feel we have moved away from the Old Testament. And I want to
try to show you in a word or two whereon that difference of inter-
pretation rests, and what is the fact that underlies it.

Open then your Old Testament again, and tell me the aspect of
nature which you most often find there. It is not the world of
sunshine and of flower. It is the world of vast and mighty things.
We read of the waves that lift themselves to heaven and of the deep
places of the unfathomed sea. The floods lift up their voice—there
is the noise of waterspouts—the stormy wind is the chariot of God.
Did thunder reverberate among the mountains? Did the earth reel
and tremble in the earthquake? The Jew was awestruck and worshiped and adored and said it was the voice of the Almighty. Did
any cedar of Lebanon overtop its neighbors? To the Jew it was the
cedar of Jehovah. Was any river very strong and swift? That was
the river of God in Jewish speech. In things that were greater and
grander than all others, in hurricane and storm, in wild and unmas-
tered forces—it was in these preeminently that the Jew awoke to the
presence and the power of God. Now turn to the teaching of the
man of Nazareth—"Consider the lilies of the field." The kingdom
of heaven is like the crash of thunder? Not so; the kingdom of
heaven is like a mustard-seed. Behold the whirlwind cleaving the
rocks apart—ah, that would have been typically Jewish; but Jesus

said, Behold the sower, in the glad morning, going out to sow. It is no longer the things that tower aloft; it is no longer the things that shock or startle—it is not *these* that to the man of Nazareth are richest in divine significancy. It is the vineyard on the sunny hill; it is the lily waving in the field. It is things common and usual and silent which no one had had eyes to see before.

Now do you see the meaning of that change? Do you think you grasp wherein the difference lies? It lies not in an altered thought of beauty but in an altered thought of the character of God. Tell me that God is the almighty King, and I look for His power in the war of elements. Tell me that His voice is that of Sinai, and it takes the grandest music of the hills to echo it. But tell me that God in heaven is my Father—that I am His child, and that He loves me dearly— and from that moment I look with other eyes on the sunshine and the streamlet and the flower. It is not in terrible or startling things that love delights to body itself forth. Never is love richer in revelation than when it consecrates all that is quiet and lowly. And it was because God was love to Jesus Christ, that when He went abroad into the world of nature, He saw God and His kingdom in the birds and in the thousand lilies of the field. The kind of God you really believe in determines mightily your thought of heaven. And the kind of God you really believe in determines mightily your thought of earth. And this is the gladness of the knowledge of God that has been given us by Christ our Savior, that it sets every common bush afire with Him and finds Him in every lily of the field.

And now in closing let me say one thing more, which helps to illuminate the mind of Christ. It is how often, when He speaks of nature, He deliberately brings man upon the scene. There are painters who delight in picturing still life, and who never introduce the human figure. They have no interest in the play of character; their genius seeks no other scope than nature. But Jesus is no painter of still life. He loves to have living forms upon the scene. He does not regard man as an intrusion but always as the completion of the picture. Think of the day when He stood by the Temple gate and looked up at the vine that was sculptured there.[4] That vine was an artist's study in still life, and it was very beautiful and perfect. But "I am the vine," said Christ, "ye are the branches," and the husbandman appears with his sharp pruning-knife. The sculpture was insufficient for the Master, until it flashed into full significance in

---

4. See David Smith, *Days of His Flesh*, 46:453.

man. In the same way when He walked abroad, He saw more than the lights and shadows of the fields. "Behold the sower"—somehow He could not rest until he had brought a living man into the picture. And so when He wandered by the Sea of Galilee and watched the waters and listened to the waves, all that, however beautiful, could not content Him until the fishermen and their nets were in the picture.[5] He could not listen to the chattering sparrows but He saw the human hands that bought and sold them. He could not look at the lilies of the field but He saw Solomon in all his glory. And it all means that while the love of nature was one of the deepest passions in Christ's heart, it was not a love that led to isolation but found its crowning in the love of man. My brother, there is a way of loving nature that chills a little the feeling for mankind. There is a passion for beauty that may be a snare, for it weakens the ties that bind us to humanity. But when a man loves nature as Jesus Christ loved nature, it will deepen and purify the springs of brotherhood and issue in service that is not less loyal because the music of hill and dale is in it.

---

5. See Dorothy Wordsworth, *Journal of a Tour made in Scotland*: "Sept. 1st. After we had wound for some time through the valley (the Pass of Awe), having met neither foot-traveler, horse, nor cart, we started at the sight of a single vessel. . . . I cannot express what romantic images this vessel brought along with her— how much more beautiful the mountains appeared, the lake how much more graceful. There was one man on board."

In hell he lifted up his eyes, being in torments (Luke 16:23).

17

The Fatal Power of Inattention

There is a well-known picture by Gustave Doré,[1] which portrays this parable of the rich man and the beggar. We are shown the rich man in the midst of Oriental luxury, and at the foot of the marble steps the diseased Lazarus. So far the picture is worthy of the genius, for it is vivid and full of rich imagination; but Doré has introduced one other feature which shows that he has misread the Savior's story. Over the beggar an Eastern slave is bending with a scourge of twigs in his uplifted hand. He has been bidden drive Lazarus away, for his misery is as a death's-head at the feast. And Doré is wrong in introducing that, for our Lord does not hint that Dives was disturbed—he was not consciously and deliberately cruel; he was only totally and hopelessly indifferent. What wrought the ruin of that pleasure-lover was not inhumanity so much as inattention. It was the fatal power of inattention that drove his barque on to the reef of woe. And on that fatal power of inattention, so strikingly and signally portrayed here, I want to speak a word or two tonight.

I do so under a sense that it is needed because that heedless spirit is so common. The attitude of innumerable people toward the great

---

1. (Paul) Gustave Doré (1832?–1883), French painter, illustrator, and sculptor.

105

questions of the religious life is just the inattentive attitude of the rich man to Lazarus at his gate. There was a time when unbelief was militant, and when men were in arms against the cause of Christ; a time when Voltaire[2] could write "Scratch out the Infamous," and the Infamous was the Redeemer of the world. But you find few militant atheists today—they are like voices crying in the wilderness; what you *do* find is something far more deadly, it is that height of insult which we call inattention. It is better sometimes to hate than to ignore, for there is at least something positive in hatred. There is hope in the foeman worthy of the steel that some day he may prove a worthy friend. But the man who takes his ease and pays no heed is the most difficult of all to deal with; and such is the common temper of today. I have many acquaintances who never come to church, and some who have told me that they never pray. I can hardly think of one among them all who is the defined antagonist of Christ. They are simply inattentive to His claims and spend their days in utter unconcern, disregarding His presence as completely as Dives disregarded that of Lazarus.

How perilous the inattentive spirit is we have only to open our eyes to see. It is one of the lessons that reach us every day as we walk through the crowded streets of a great city. Readers of Marcus Aurelius[3] will remember how he bases the art of life upon attention.[4] In the jostle and pressure of a modern city, that truth has a very literal significance. Well could I understand the Highland crofter[5] moving across the moor-land inattentively. There is nothing within hail except the sheep and the whirring bird that is startled at his tread. But for a man who lives in Glasgow or in London, to move inattentive amid the rush of traffic is to augment by a thousandfold the perils that are inevitable where life is swift and full. Not a day passes but in the city of London someone is maimed through being inattentive. I might put it in an even grimmer fashion, for every day in the streets someone is killed. They were not drunk nor were they seeking death; I do not know what the coroner may say about them,

---

2. Voltaire (1694–1778), French philosopher, historian, dramatist, and essayist.

3. Marcus Aurelius (A.D. 121–180), Stoic philosopher and writer, emperor of Rome (A.D. 161–180).

4. I mean that as a first condition of "the wrestler's art"—the art of life—the Emperor over and over again insists upon attention, e.g. 6:53; 7:4; 8:22, etc. This is as true of the "great style" as of great living; see Sir J. Reynold's *Fifteen Discourses*, 3.

5. tenant farmer

but I know that a true verdict would be this: Slain through the fatal power of inattention. Now all that happens not where life is meager, but where life is rich and tumultuous and full. Nowhere is it so perilous to be indifferent as within the sweep of mighty tides of life. And if the life that is revealed in Christ is mightier in its flow than that of Babylon, do you not feel the risks of inattention when that life is at your very door?

Again we might throw light upon the matter by considering the common laws of health. There are certain principles with which we are all familiar and to which we give the name of laws of health. They are written upon the framework of our bodies; they are not many nor are they hard to keep; but they are as certainly the laws of God as any commandment graven in the decalogue. Now you never meet a man who hates these laws or breaks them in a spirit of rebellion. But you meet many who are inattentive and who constantly and recklessly neglect them. And I ask the doctors here whether that inattention is not a rash and perilous behavior and is not certain in the course of years to bring the body of a man to ruin? You do not need to defy the laws of health to have the body taking vengeance on you. The body avenges far more than defiance; it inevitably avenges inattention. Many a man yet living is in hell and lifts up his eyes toward heaven being in torments; and at the back of all his torments is not vice but a persistent and foolish disregard. Now if confessedly that is true of the body, is it incredible that it should hold true of the soul? Are you certain to escape in spiritual things for a line of action that never escapes in physical? On the contrary, the higher that we rise, the more are we likely to suffer for neglect, just because the interests involved are of such tremendous and eternal consequence.

Before passing from this aspect, I should like to say that this is one of the ministries of pain. Whatever other functions pain may have, one is that it serves to fix attention. If there is anything harmful working in the body, it is supremely important that it should be localized, and so comes pain and rings the alarm bell and concentrates attention on the spot. Pain is the bugle sounding the reveille. Pain is the watchman crying on the walls. We should sleep on while the foe took the citadel were we not roused by the trumpet blast of pain. And though it is hard thus to be roused sometimes, and we are prone to murmur at the summons, yet better, surely, to be rudely wakened than to be beaten by an insidious foe. We shall never grasp some of God's dealings with us unless we class them with that call of pain. Sometimes it were cruel to let us sleep; sometimes the only kindness is to wake us. And there are sorrows and failures and bitter disappointments which we can never hope to understand, until we realize they are God's stratagems to fix our attention on the things which matter.

I wish now to say a word or two on some of the causes of this inattention, and perhaps the most common cause of all is custom. Someone has said that if all the stars ceased shining and then after a hundred years shone out again, there is not an eye but would be lifted heavenward, and not a lip but would break forth in praise. But the stars were shining when we were little children, and they are there tonight and will be there tomorrow, and we are so accustomed to that glory that we rarely give to it a single thought. What eyes we have when we travel on the Continent! Every river and hill and castle we observe. But in Glasgow and by the banks of Clyde,[6] a district rich in story and in beauty, *there* we are so accustomed to the scenery that we have eyes for nothing but the newspaper. "One good custom doth corrupt the world,"[7] and it does so, because it lulls to sleep. It is a bad thing to grow accustomed to the wrong. It may be worse to grow accustomed to the right. And that is why in the history of the church God sends the earthquake and the crash of storm, that men may be roused and startled to concern and escape the fatal sway of inattention.

Another cause of inattention is a lowered vitality. I think we have all had experience of that. When we are weary and the flame of life is low, somehow we can neither grasp nor grip. Everything becomes formless and elusive. We read and hardly understand the page; we work yet seem to master nothing; we pray and might be praying to a shadow. Then comes the morning, it may be in the springtime, when the life within us is strong and full again. We are quickened to the finest fibers of our being, and it is a pure joy to be alive. And at once, in that renewed vitality, we grow alert, attentive, able to grasp and grip; not a page but is radiant with meaning now, not a thing but has a thought behind it. "I am come to give abundant life," says Christ, and to give it here and now and not tomorrow. Do you not see, then, how fellowship with Christ wakens a man's attention to the highest? It is in that life which may be yours tonight, and for which you do not need to

6. The Clyde River in southern Scotland.
7. From "In Memoriam A.H.H." by Tennyson.

wait until springtime, that you can seize with an attentive faith the things that are unseen and eternal.

But the deepest cause of inattention is still to seek. The deepest cause of it is lack of love. Let a man once love a book, a land, a woman, and he will never be inattentive any more. When a young man is paying court to somebody, do not the people say "he is paying her attention"? Love and attention, in the people's speech, have practically the same signification. It was love that made the father of the prodigal so quick to discern the figure of his son. It was love that made our Savior give such heed to the cry of the blind beggar by the road. And it is love to Christ which wakens the dulled heart not only to the things that are unseen, but to the infinite value of the soul that is lodged under the raggedness of Lazarus. "Simon, son of Jonas, lovest thou Me"—that was the threefold question of the Master. Only when *that* was clearly ascertained, was there given the commandment, "Feed My sheep." For love is quick to see the need of others and to read what is hidden from a thousand eyes, and to discern beyond the veil the things that matter; for only he who loves, knows God.

Is there a God beside Me? (Isa. 44:8).

18

The Immanence of God

In the Christian view of God there are two attributes which it is not easy for the human reason to combine. One of them we call the transcendence of God; to the other we give the name of immanence.

Now what do we mean by the divine transcendence? We mean that God is over all, blessed forever. We mean that apart from and above the universe, there lives and reigns a personal Creator. We mean that were this world to be extinguished and were every living being to disappear, still would there be, eternal in the heavens, the Spirit whom we designate as God. Over against all created things, sustaining them and yet distinct from them, self-conscious in the silence of eternity, and looking from without on all things made—it is to such a God, exalted over all, that we apply the attribute transcendence.

And what do we mean by the immanence of God? We mean the presence of the Almighty in creation. We mean that time and space and all their thousand occupants are but the garments that we see Him by. Deep through the universe runs the thrill of life, and wheresoever that life is, there is God. His personal habits are the laws of nature; His love of beauty is seen in every valley. It is He who awakes in the waking of the spring; it is He who moves in the torrent and the tide; it is He who rises to the joy of consciousness in the consciousness of His highest creature man. A God transcendent, like some consum-

110

mate painter, adorns with His brush the lilies of the field; but a God who is immanent breathes into the lilies, and they become the expression of Himself. A God transcendent, like some master-craftsman, fashions the fowls of the air for flight; but a God who is immanent lives in every bird and breaks the eternal silence in their song. A God transcendent, like some mighty sculptor, models with His deft hand the human form; but a God who is immanent looks through human eyes and thinks in the thinking of the human brain.

Now at different times in the history of man these differing attributes have received special prominence. Sometimes the stress has been laid upon transcendence; at other times upon the immanence. Thus, for example, in the reign of Calvinism, it was divine transcendence that was in the forefront. High over space and time and life and death there sat the immutable and sovereign God; and much of the noble massiveness of Calvinism and its power of forming large and kingly character sprang from its reasoned yet passionate insistence on the eternal sovereignty of God. Calvinism has not been rich in poets, unless it kindled them, as it did Burns, into rebellion. But Calvinism has had extraordinary power in creating a character of rectitude and weight. And this it has mainly done by its two messages, its laying "in the dust life's glory dead," and its exalting into the heaven of heavens the immutable, sovereign, and transcendent God.

But today it is not transcendence that is potent. The pendulum has swung round to the other side. Today it is the immanence of God that is claiming the chief thought of Western Christendom. It is on the immanence of God that men insist who profess to be leading the march of human thought. It is not God above us, it is God within us, that is the watchword of the latest systems. And it is deeply interesting to discover what is the meaning of this revolution, and what are the causes that have led to it.

Well, then, if I mistake not, the chief causes of this change are two. The one is the devotion of our age to science, and the other is the modern delight in nature. Our fathers thought far more of heaven than we do. It is not heaven men study now—it is the earth. With splendid devotion men have been studying nature, learning her laws, discovering her methods; and then when we were in danger of forgetting the wonder and the gladness of it all, there have come the poets with their anointed eyes and shown us what was behind the veil. It is not theologians who have been most powerful in altering the emphasis in our thought of God. It has been men like Wordsworth in the sphere of poetry and men like Darwin[1] in the sphere of science. For the one has taught us to feel the mystic presence that broods in the lonely places of the world; and the other has shown us in orchid and in earthworm an exquisite and unfathomable wisdom. That is why there is such intense interest now in any theology that proclaims God's immanence. It precisely meets the Spirit of an age that has been trained and taught as ours has been. Not in the heavens, it cries, and not beyond the stars, but here, where the earth is war, and human hearts are beating; here, in the purpose and progress of humanity, here, and here only, know we God.

Now I am far too much the child of my own age not to have felt the power of that appeal. It is one of the most subtle and captivating doctrines that ever entered into the heart of man. The world no more can be a barren place, if in every hedgerow there is the thrill of God. The sorriest outcast seems clad in a new glory, if his life be but a mode of the divine. And if God be sleeping in mountain and in sea and wakening into consciousness in man, does it not make the story of the universe a story of incomparable grandeur? For all its charm, I do not hesitate to say that the loss in such a conception is incalculable. Deny, reject, make light of God's transcendence, and you cut at the very roots of human progress. The immanence of God is a great truth to be grasped firmly by the believing soul; but to say that the immanence of God is everything is to be a traitor to tomorrow. Let me try to show you some results that follow when we identify the Almighty with His universe. You may call it pantheism, or you may deny that name; we are not here debating about names. I only want to make patent what must issue if you confine the Almighty to His world and say, "There is no God, save the God who breathes in our humanity."

First, then, when we deny transcendence, we cease to have a God who is a person. The God of the pantheist may be a flowing stream; He certainly is not a living spirit. You remember how the exiled psalmist cried, " My soul thirsteth for the living God." It was for the *living* God that he was craving with a deep and unappeasable desire. And the one thing that you blot out of the universe when you identify the Creator with His creatures is a God who will answer when His children speak—a living and communicating God. Sooner or later, there come times to all of us when our deepest need is for the living God. It may be in times of suffering that we need Him; it may be in

---

1. Charles Darwin (1809–1882), English naturalist and author.

bereavement or in sin. But in such hours, if we allowed ourselves the thought that there was no one who cared or knew upon the throne, the burdens and the cares of life would grow insufferable, and we should be plunged in an abyss of darkness. But there is not, and there cannot be, a living God, if God be but the Spirit of the universe. You can adore the movement of creation, but you cannot cry to it, "Father, I have sinned." We do not want to find ourselves divine in the great moments when we are most ourselves. We want to find the living God above us, who is ready to hear us when we call.

The fact is that in bringing God so near, the pantheist really puts Him far away. Being what we are, God is truly nearest when He is seated on His throne in heaven. I am not always nearest those around me save in a shallow and corporeal sense. Those that are nearest may be a thousand miles off, if so be that they love and understand me. And so with God in the altitude of heaven—if He knows and cares and understands and pities, then is He far nearer to my heart than if He were personless and by my side. You seem to bring God within my very grasp when you tell me that His life is in the violet. If His presence is interfused with setting suns, you seem to bring Him under my very gaze. But if that be all—if He be nowhere else—if you must search for Him beyond the universe in vain, then the divine is brought within our hail, only to be banished far away. It is not *things*, whatever be their essence, that can enter through the portals of the heart. It is personality and love and power. It is the influence of a living spirit. And all these you inevitably forfeit when you believe only in God's immanence, which robs the heart of the God for whom it craves, while it seems to bring Him very near.

Again, the popular pantheism of today is also fatal to human personality. When you lose the personality of God, you lose the individuality of man. Whatever charges men leveled against Calvinism, none ever hinted that it weakened character. Faced by a sovereign and transcendent God, men were strengthened to do and to endure. And it is when you lose that sense of the high God and merge Him in the movement of His world, that you lose the presence above us and beyond us that is so needful to draw us to our best. Slip the anchor of the living God, and you slip the anchor of accountability. I am but a mood or moment of the infinite—a wave upon the sea which is divine. And sooner or later, as that conception strengthens, the meaning of personality decays, and men forget, insensibly but surely, much of their noblest heritage in Christ. It is not by telling a man he is divine that you help him toward a better

manhood. It is by telling him that above him is a God who loves
him and to whom he is responsible. But you never can proclaim
that truth again, if God is only immanent in nature; nor will all the
new significance of nature atone for the irremediable loss.

Once more, the popular pantheism of today is certain to put our
moral life in jeopardy, for it destroys, and must inevitably destroy,
the sharp distinction between good and evil. The moral power of
the cross of Christ has operated in a twofold way. It has not only
made goodness very beautiful. It has also made sin exceeding sinful. A man may be a Christian though he parts with much that was
regarded as vital by the fathers; but no man can ever be a Christian
who treats sin in a light and easy way. "God commended His own
love to us in that while we were yet *sinners*, Christ died for us. The
meaning of that love will grow or lessen, according to our measurement of sin. And hence it is that when men have most deeply felt
the wonder of the love of God in Christ, they have felt at the same
time the guilt of sin and known that it was exceeding sinful.

Now it is just that moral heritage that is likely to be lost in the
teaching of today. It is a bad thing to vilify humanity; I believe it is
even worse to deify it. If the life of God be the life of the human race
and the activity of God be man's activity, where is your standard to
tell that *this* is right and to say with authority that *that* is wrong? No
man can by searching find out God, and if God be but the flowing
tide of life, then all the foam of it and every crest must share in the
attributes of the divine. It is one God who loves in a St. John and
thinks in the atrocities of Nero. It is one God who reigns in a Victoria
and in that choice instrument the Sultan. It is one God who inspires
the toiler who is helping to raise his brother in the slums and who
breathes, with a breath that is divine, in the degrading passions of the
libertine. If God's activity be our activity—if God's intelligence be
our intelligence—if God be the substance at the back of all things,
becoming conscious in the life of man—then everything in us must
be in God, and evil at the worst is limitation. Water is water, whether
in the marsh or in the unfathomable depths of ocean. And God is God
in a Richard[2] or a Tamerlane,[3] as surely as in a Thomas à Kempis.[4]

---

2. Kings of England: Richard I, 1157–1199; Richard II, 1367–1400; Richard
III, 1452–1485.

3. Tamerlane (1336?–1405), Tartar conqueror in southern and western Asia,
ruler of Tamarkand, 1369–1405.

4. Thomas à Kempis (1379?–1471), German ecclesiastic and author.

But some one may perhaps say what about conscience—is there not always left the voice of conscience? To which we would answer, as Knox[5] did to Mary,[6] "Conscience, madam, requires to be educated." The way that some people talk about their conscience is enough to try the patience of a saint. You would think that conscience could live and do its work regardless of the atmosphere it breathed. Whereas the fact is that in all our being there is no faculty that needs more to be fed, and none that more certainly will fail to answer, when it is deliberately starved. A tender girl will feel more pangs of conscience when she has committed some trifling misdemeanor, than a hardened criminal will ever feel when he breaks the plainest law of God. There are many people who scorn the name of Christian, and who say, I am content to follow conscience; yet if they only knew it, that conscience which they trust is hopelessly in debt to Jesus Christ. For it has been nurtured through ages upon Christian truth and made tender through the wealth of Christian feeling, and if it is strong and vigorous today, it owes its power largely to its heritage. We may picture conscience as a simple thing, but conscience is very far from being simple. It is no more simple than the ear is simple—that outward organ for the voice of God. It has been educated through the stress of years; it has been taught by the sacrifice and love of ages; and it still responds for a period of time to the calling of a faith that is disowned. You remember how Elijah, fed with angels' food, went in the strength of that nurture forty days. There is many a conscience like the journeying prophet, still active because fed from heaven yesterday. But the day must come when conscience will grow weak and fail to pronounce its verdict with authority, unless it is fed again with that same nourishment that has kept it strong and tender to this hour. There is nothing in an exclusive immanence that has any power to reinforce the conscience. There is no law with its divine "Thou shalt not." There is no atonement on the cross for guilt. There is no Spirit of a holy God sent in Christ's power to convince of sin. Pantheism may be full of charm, like the faint mist upon the Highland hills, but slowly and surely, confusing good with evil, it saps the foundations of the conscience.

And not only so, but, as has often been noted, the logical outcome is this, that might is right. If God and the life of His

---

5. John Knox (c. 1510–1572), Scottish Protestant reformer.
6. Mary I "Bloody Mary" (1516–1558), Queen of England.

universe be one, then the mightier the life, the more of God. "The vanquished party," says a famous Frenchman[7]—"The vanquished party always deserves to be vanquished. It is time that the philosophy of history put an end to the declamations of philanthropy." Lovers of Shakespeare love him not the least for the triumphal marches he sounds over the fallen.[8] It is not always the victor to whom he gives the crown; Shakespeare has crowns for the baffled and the beaten. Yet never again for any beaten man will there be the echo of victorious music, if there is nothing divine—no God, no goal—except the evolving spirit of the universe. It was inevitable that a thinker like Carlyle[9] should come to believe as he did in hero-worship. A hero may be good, he may be bad—the one essential is that he be strong. There is no room for the baffled and the weak—no place for the useless, the beaten, and the fallen—in a world whose god is but a stream of being which neither can pity nor can love.

From all such thoughts, whatever be their charm, let us come back to the Fatherhood of God. Let us learn anew the meaning of the prayer, "Our Father which art in heaven." Christ's revelation of God was that of fatherhood, and so long as we are true to that, we have a living and true God who meets the deepest need of human hearts. There is transcendence in the thought of fatherhood—the sweet and perfect sovereignty of love. Above His children, strong and just and merciful, a refuge from the storm, there stands the Father. And in fatherhood no less is immanence, for the father's very life is in the child, and in ways not less real because they are undefinable, father and child are one. All that is noblest in the thought of sovereignty, all that is fairest in the thought of immanence meets in that God whose name and nature have been revealed to us by and in the Lord. We beseech Thee, then, O God, show us Thy glory. Give us the spirit that cries, "Abba, Father." Then earth and humanity will not be less because the life of the Divine is more.

---

7. Cousin, *History of Modern Philosophy* (1852), 1:186–9.

8. see Dowden, *Shakespeare* (1892), p. 159.

9. Thomas Carlyle (1795–1861), Scottish essayist and historian.

He gave them drink as out of the great
depths (Ps. 78:15).

19

Drink from the Depths

The psalmist is here reviewing the providence of God that sustained the children of Israel in the desert. That providence had made a deep impression on him, and he delights to dwell upon its wonders. There is a sense, I believe, in which the poet is really the best of all historians. He sees, by the gift of a trained imagination, into the heart of men and the character of movements. And though he may lack the minute and critical knowledge that is in the keeping of laborious students, yet he often brings us nearer to the truth than the man who discovers and refutes his errors. One often feels that it is so with the psalmist, and especially when he is dealing with the Exodus. For him the miracles that marked that journey were not isolated and solitary splendors. They were rather the discoveries of that power which is everywhere present and everywhere upholding; only in other lives they are writ small, while here in the Exodus they are writ large.

Take for example the water from the rock of which the psalmist is speaking in our text. It comes to him in a flash, as the great wonder of it, that God gave them drink as out of the great depths. He sees the Israelites crowding around the rock and saying in their hearts, "This cannot last long." He sees them watching for the supply to fail, as, of course, coming from a rock it must soon do. And then he sees their look of wild surprise when it dawns on them that the stream is inexhaustible and is fed by channels they know nothing of, from boundless and unfathomable reservoirs. What the people crave for is a draught of water, and God in His mercy gives them their desire. But He fills their cups, not from a little cistern, but as from some illimitable ocean. And the psalmist knows that that is always true, for whenever the Almighty satisfies His creatures, He gives them drink as out of the great depths. On that thought I wish to dwell tonight, carrying it through some of the activities of God.

Think, then, for a moment of the world of nature as it unfolds itself in all its beauty round us. There is not a bird or beast, there is not a tree or flower but is ministered to in the way our text describes. I take the tiniest weed that roots among the stones—the flower in the crannied wall of which the poet speaks—and I ask, what does it need to live; what does it need that it may flower and fruit? The answer is that it needs a little warmth; it needs an occasional moistening with rain. Now in a certain measure that is true, but you can never stop there in this mysterious universe. At the back of the warmth which it needs, there is the sun; and at the back of every raindrop, there is sky and ocean; and it takes sun and sea and the white cloud of heaven to satisfy that tiniest weed among the stones, which comes to its delicate beauty unregarded and may be crushed by any passing foot. Try to explain the light that a rose needs, and you are carried into the depths of solar energy. Look at the raindrop on the hawthorn hedge—has it not been drawn "out of the boundless deep"? And so there is not a rose in any garden nor a leaf that unfolds itself on any tree but is ever whispering to the hearing ear, "He gave me drink as out of the great depths."

Again, think of our senses for a moment—think of our sight and hearing, for example. One of the plainest facts about our senses is the different way they translate what they receive. To one man, as to the Peter Bell of Wordsworth, a primrose is just a primrose and no more.[1] To another, in the meanest flower that blows there are thoughts that do often lie too deep for tears. And it is not the eye alone that differentiates, it is the life that is hidden deep behind the eye; He giveth them drink as out of the great depths. Or two men listen to a piece of music, and one, as he listens, is profoundly stirred by it. There seem to pass before him, as he listens, visions of what is high and fair and beautiful. And he hears the calling of his

---

1. "Peter Bell" (1819) by Wordsworth.

brightest hopes and the cry of regret for all his wasted years and the stooping over him again of angel faces that he has loved long since and lost awhile.[2] All this is kindled in some hearts by music—this burning of hope and haunting of regret; yet play that very piece before another, and it is sound and fury, signifying nothing.[3] Is not the ear of a dead person perfect? Is not every membrane and convolution there? Yet call to it, or whisper to it passionately, will it play its part and carry the news of love? Yesterday there would have been a smile of recognition; there is not a flicker of response today. So at the back of every sense we have there is a deep that you can never fathom. All that a man is, looks through his eyes. All that his soul is, listens through his ears. If the eye could speak or if the ear could speak, would they not echo the language of the text, "He gave us drink as out of the great depths."

Again let us think for a moment of God's ways in providence—in the ordering and discipline of our lives. One of the lessons we learn as we grow older is that our discipline is not exceptional. When we are young our joys are all our own; we never dream that others can have known them. When we are young we take our little sorrows as if there were no such sorrows in the world. And much of the bitterness of childish trial lies in its terrible sense of isolation, in the feeling that in the whole wide world there is no one who has had to suffer just like us. It seems as if God had cut a special channel for us out of which no other life had ever drunk. In joy and grief, in sunshine and in shadow, we seem to move apart when we are children. But as life advances and our outlook broadens and we learn the story of the lives around us, then do we see that we are not alone but are being made to drink of the great depths. It is not by exceptional providences that we live. It not by exceptional joys we are enriched. It is not by anything rare or strange or singular that we are fashioned under the hand of God. It is by sorrows that are as old as man, by trials that a thousand hearts have felt, by joys that are common as the wind is common that breathes on the palace and on the meanest street. By these things do we live; by these we grow—by love and tears, by trials, by work, by death—by the things that link us all into a brotherhood, the things that are common to ten thousand hearts. And it is when we come to recognize that truth and to feel our comradeship within a common discipline, that we say, as the psalmist said of Israel, "He gave us drink as out of the great depths."

2. Cardinal Newman (1801–1890), "Lead Kindly Light" (1833).

3. From *Macbeth* by Shakespeare.

Then think again for a moment of the Bible. Now there is one thing that always arrests me in the Bible. It is that the Bible is such an ancient book and yet is so intensely modern and practical. Think of the ages which have gone since it was written and how "heaven and earth have passed away" since then; think of our cities and of the life we live in them and of the stress and strain unknown in the quiet East; to me it is wonderful, when I reflect on that, that the Bible should be of any use at all now and should not have moved into the quiet of libraries to be the joy of the unworldly scholar. But if there is one thing certain it is this, that the Bible meets the need of modern life. In spite of all criticism—and I rejoice in criticism—as a practical guide there is no book to touch it. There is not a problem you are called to face and not a duty you are called to do, there is not a cross you are compelled to carry and not a burden you are forced to bear, but your strength for it all shall be as the strength of ten, if you make a daily companion of your Bible. Now this is what you feel about the Bible, that it never offers a draught from shallow waters. You do not find there a set of petty maxims, but you find the everlasting love of God there. You do not find any shallow views of sin there, but a Lamb slain from the foundation of the world. And *that* is the secret of the Bible's permanence, when our little systems have had their day and ceased to be, that for sin and sorrow and life and death and duty, it gives us to drink as out of the great depths.

Then lastly, think for a moment upon Jesus—of Jesus in relation to His words. If ever words were as water to a thirsty world, surely it was the words that Jesus spoke. How simple they were, and yet how deep! How tender and full of love, and yet how searching! They seemed to pierce into the very heart, until a man felt that his secret thought was known. Now there are men whose lives so contradict their words that when you know the men you cannot listen to them. And there are men who are so much less than their own words that when you come to know them you are disappointed. But what people felt about Jesus Christ was this, that when all was uttered, the half was never told, for at the back of all His words there was *Himself*, deeper unfathomably than His deepest speech. That is why the words of Christ will live even when heaven and earth have passed away. You can exhaust the cup or drain the goblet dry, but you cannot exhaust the spring fed from the deeps. And just because the words of Jesus Christ spring from the depths of that divine humanity, they will save and strengthen the obedient heart to the last recorded syllable of time.

He that observeth the wind shall not sow;
and he that regardeth the clouds shall not
reap (Eccl. 11:4).

20

The Fault of Over-Prudence

The language in which this proverb is couched is taken from the harvest-field and is therefore peculiarly applicable at this season,[1] "He that observeth the wind shall not sow; and he that regardeth the clouds shall not reap." That does not mean, of course, that the way to succeed in farming is entirely to disregard the weather. There are climatic conditions in which if a man harvested, he would instantly write himself down a madman. But it means that if a farmer will not work save when all the conditions for his work are perfect; if he is always doubting and fearing and forecasting rain, worrying and fretting instead of making the best of things; then probably he will neither sow nor reap and is little likely to make a successful farmer. Constituted as this world is, one must be instant in season and out of season. Just as a man may fail through too much zeal, so may a man fail through too much prudence. And it is upon that fault of over-prudence, as crystallized in the proverb of our text, that I wish to speak a word or two this evening.

In the first place, I like to apply our text to the important matter of our bodily health. If a man is always thinking of his health, the

1. Preached in the autumn.

121

chances are he will have a sorry harvest. That we must be reasonably careful of our bodies, we all know; it is one of the plainest of our Christian duties. By the coming of the Son of God in our flesh and by making the body the temple of the Spirit, by the great doctrine of the resurrection when what is sown in weakness shall be raised in glory, the Gospel of Christ has glorified the body in a way that even the Greeks had never dreamed of. But I am not speaking just now of reasonable care; I am speaking of morbid and worrying anxiety. Why, you can hardly drink a glass of milk today but some newspaper will warn you that you may be poisoned. And what I want you to feel is that that alarmist attitude, which will scarce allow you to breathe in this glad world, is the kind of thing that is denounced by Solomon in the memorable proverb of this verse. So far as I have ever studied Christian Science, there is not a little in it that seems to me absurd, but there is one thing that seems entirely admirable and that is its refusal to let a man brood on what he suffers. There are people who actually seem to wish you ill again, they are so bent on recalling your old illnesses; but there is no worse service you can do a man than to drag his tortured past out of its grave. "Let the dead bury its dead; follow thou Me." Lean on the Keeper of Israel and go forward. He that observes the wind shall not sow; and he that regards the clouds shall not reap.

Again, I like to apply our text to the difficulties that beset our daily work, for we may so fix our eyes upon these difficulties, that all the strength is taken from the arm. A man may ruin any work by rashness, as Simon Peter would have ruined the work of Jesus; but remember that if the rash man has his perils, there are also perils for the over-prudent. Do you recall the parable of the talents? Do you remember why the man with the one talent failed? "I was afraid," he said, "for I knew thou wert an hard man, and so I buried my talent in the earth." The other servants took the common risks in giving out their money to the changers; but this man would risk absolutely nothing, and, willing to risk nothing, he lost all. Do you imagine it is just a chance that the man who acted so had the one talent? We talk a deal about the perils of genius, but our Savior talked of those of mediocrity. Great men have got their glow and inspiration; things are worth doing when you can do them greatly. There is an ease about a master-mind that turns the very toil into delight. Genius is prodigal and scatters its pearls abroad; genius, like childhood, is equal to its problem. It is men of the one talent and mediocre mind who are tempted to the sin of over-prudence. I have known so many average men who failed because they were waiting for an impossible perfection. They said "Tomorrow—by and by—I shall be ready; I shall have all the information in ten years"—and the ten years hurried by, and they did nothing, except to wish that they had started earlier. Do you think we ministers could ever preach to you if we observed the winds and regarded the clouds? If we waited for inspiration and a glowing brain, could we ever face the inevitable Sunday? The hours will come, and come to every man, when task-work quivers and palpitates with life; but perhaps they only come because we have been faithful, with a certain grimness, through the days of gloom. Let a man hold to his lifework through mood and melancholy. Let him hold to it through headache and through heartache.[2] For he that observes the wind will never sow; and he that regards the clouds will never reap.

Again, I would apply our text to moral effort and to the battles we fight against besetting sins. Sometimes in such hours we fail through recklessness, but far more often through some overprudence. What is your special and peculiar weakness? Many of you could say in an instant what it was; and you have had hours when you were so ashamed of it that you determined to make a fight for liberty. Now if in that God-sent and decisive hour you had acted resolutely and immediately; if you had shut your eyes to everything save this, that at all costs that besetting sin must go, how different would the years have been for you! But what did you do? You looked before and after; you thought too precisely on the event, as Hamlet says. You thought of your friends, of your past failures, of tomorrow—of everything that could discourage and depress you; until you lost all heart to take the plunge, and tonight you are farther off from it than ever. There are times when it is folly to observe the winds. There are times when it is madness to regard the clouds. Past failures—all that your friends may say—"What is that to thee? Follow thou Me." In all high venture there is a glorious blindness—blindness to everything except the beckoning hand.

Again, our text has notable application in the great work of national reform. A certain disregard of obvious difficulties and of all that would discourage lesser spirits has ever been one mark of

---

2. *E.g.* Sir Walter Scott's *Journal*, July 2, 1828: "I am at any rate very ill today with a rheumatic headache, and a still more vile hypochondriacal affection, which fills my head with pain, my heart with sadness, and my eyes with tears. . . . I wrought therefore, and endured all this forenoon.

great reformers whether in the church or in the state. When told that
Duke George of Saxony was lying in wait for him, "I would go,"
said Luther,[3] "if it rained Duke Georges." When told that the devil
would catch him if he went to the diet,[4] "I would go if there were as
many devils in Worms as there are tiles upon the housetops." The
winds were bitter and the clouds black as midnight, and Luther
sowed and reaped because he disregarded them. Those of you who
know the story of the Scottish Reformation will remember a similar
incident in the life of Knox. It was in 1559 when, traveling by the
coast of Fife, Knox met a few of the reforming nobles at St.
Andrews. He intimated that he would preach in the cathedral, and
when the Roman Catholic archbishop heard of his intention, he sent
Knox word that if he dared to preach he would have him shot in the
pulpit by his soldiery. Everything was done to dissuade Knox from
his purpose, but nothing could make the least impression on him.
He recalled the day when, a prisoner in the galley, he had prophe-
sied that he would preach the gospel there. And so he preached, and
not a shot was fired—he preached on Christ putting out the traders
from the temple; and in a day or two St. Andrews, magistrates and
all, had come out on the side of the evangel.[5] That was the spirit
which gave us a free Scotland, a spirit which could disregard the
clouds. And that is the spirit which is needed still if we are to sweep
away our national iniquities. It is an easy thing to sneer at the
fanatic and to say that he is the ruin of his cause. It is an easy thing
to make fun of the enthusiast who is so terribly in earnest that he is
not wise. But I will tell you the man who is a thousand times more
fatal to any cause in church and state than the enthusiast, and that is
the man who always eyes the clouds and spends his days in shrink-
ing from the wind. It is better to try and fail than to do nothing. We
snatch our triumphs from the brink of failure. It is so easy to stand
aside and criticize and magnify difficulties and state objections. But
we are here to sow and we are here to reap, as Luther knew and as
every brave man knows, and he that observes the wind will never
sow, and he that regards the clouds will never reap.

3. Martin Luther (1483–1546), German theologian and leader of the Protestant
Reformation in Germany.

4. a formal assembly to discuss state affairs

5. Knox, *History of the Reformation,* 2 (Laing) 1:347–50. Cf. Hamlet, 5. 2. 8:
"Our indiscretion sometimes serves us well"; and by way of contrast, Goldsmith,
Vicar of Wakefield (Globe) 4(2): "One virtue he [Mr. Wilmot] had in perfection,
which was prudence, too often the only one left us at seventy-two."

Then, lastly, I want you to apply our text to the great matter of decision for Christ Jesus. I want you to go away thinking of Peter when he walked upon the sea to get to Christ. "Lord, if it be Thou, bid me come to Thee," and Jesus across the water cried to Peter, "Come"; whereupon Peter leaped out of the ship and walked upon the water to his Lord. Then he regarded the clouds—how the wild rack was flying! He observed the wind—how boisterous it was—and so observing, he began to sink and had to cry, "Lord, save me, or I perish." Is not Christ saying "Come" to someone here tonight? Is there not someone like Peter who has heard His call? In such an hour the one thing that is fatal is to give heed to the uproar of the storm. O you of little faith, wherefore do you doubt? He is mighty to save and powerful to keep. Disregard everything except the beckoning Savior, and by and by you will reap a hundredfold.

He that is not with Me is against Me
(Matt. 12:30).

21

The Intolerance of Jesus

Our Lord had just performed a notable miracle in healing a man who was possessed of a devil. It had made a profound impression on the people and had forced the conviction that this was indeed Messiah. Unable to dispute the miracle itself, the Pharisees tried to impugn the power behind it, and in their cowardly and treacherous way they suggested that there was something demoniac about Christ. With a readiness of resource which never failed Him, Christ showed in a flash the weakness of that argument. If He was the friend and comrade of the demons, was He likely to make a brother-demon homeless? Then catching fire at these insinuations and moved to righteous anger by these slanders, He said, "He that is not with Me is against Me."

I want, then, to speak for a little while this evening on the intolerance of Jesus Christ. However startling the subject may appear and however the sound of it may jar upon us, I am convinced we shall never understand our Lord if we fail to take account of His intolerance. We have heard much of the geniality of Jesus and of the depth and range of His compassion; nor can we ever exaggerate, in warmest language, the genial and generous aspect of His character. But it is well that the listening ear should be attuned to catch the sterner

126

music of that life, lest, missing it, we miss the fine severity which goes to the perfecting of moral beauty. Wherever the spirit of Jesus is at work, there is found a sweet and masterful intolerance. The one thing that the gospel cannot do is to look with easy good-nature on the world. And if this passionate urgency of claim has ever marked the activities of Christendom, we must try to trace it to the fountain-head and find it in the character of Christ.

Of course there is an intolerance so cold and hard that it must always be alien from the Master's spirit. All that is best in us condemns the temper which lacks the redeeming touch of comprehension. When the poet Shelley[1] was a lad still in his teens, he fell violently in love with his cousin Harriet Grove. Shelley was a skeptic even then, and on account of his skepticism his cousin was removed from him. And those of you who have read his letters of that period will remember how they throb with the great hope that he might live to do battle with intolerance. Now Shelley was a poet with all a poet's ardor, yet I think that most young men have had that feeling. Nor is it one of those feelings that pass away with youth; it generally strengthens with the tale of years. "One has only to grow old," says Goethe,[2] "to become tolerant." As life advances, if we live it well, we commonly grow less rigid in our judgment. By all we have seen and suffered, all we have tried and failed in, our sympathies grow broader with the years. We learn how precious is the grace of charity; how near akin may be the fiercest combatants; how great is the allowance we must make for those of whose hidden life we know so little.

I mention that just to make plain to you that I am not shutting my eyes to common truths. Yet the fact remains that in all great personalities, there is a strain of what is called intolerance. There are things in which it must be yea or nay—the everlasting no, as Carlyle[3] has it. There are spheres in which all compromise is treachery, and when a man must say with Luther, "Here I stand." And that intolerance, so far from being the enemy of love and sympathy and generous culture, is the rock that a man needs to set his feet on, if he is to cast his rope to those who cry for help. You find it in the God

---

1. Percy Bysshe Shelley (1792–1822), English poet.

2. Johann Wolfgang von Goethe (1749–1832), German writer and philosopher, see Helps, *Companions of My Solitude*, 12 *ad fin.*

3. From *Sartor Resartus* by Thomas Carlyle (1795–1881), English philosopher and essayist.

of the Old Testament—"Thou shalt have no other gods before Me."
He is a jealous God and brooks no rival. He must be loved with
heart and soul and strength and mind. You find it in the music of
the psalmist and in the message of prophet and apostle,[4] and you
find it bosomed amid all the love that shone in the character of
Jesus Christ. Never was man so tender as the Lord. Never was man
so swift to sympathize. Never did sinners so feel that they were
understood. Never did the lost so feel that they were loved. Yet
with all that pity and grace and boundless comprehension, I say
you have never fathomed the spirit of the Master until you have
recognized within its range a certain glorious and divine intolerance. We talk of the infinite tolerance of Shakespeare; it is a commonplace of all Shakespearean criticism. Nothing was alien from
that mighty genius; the world was a stage and he knew all the
players. But underneath that worldwide comprehension there is a
scorn of scorn, a hate of hate; there is such doom on the worthless
and the wicked as can scarce be paralleled in any literature; and
until you have heard that message of severity—that judgment which
is the other side of love—you have never learned the secret of the
dramatist. In a loftier and a more spiritual sense that is true of our
Master, Jesus Christ. He loved us and He gave Himself for us. He
says to every weary heart, "Come unto Me." But that same spirit
which was so true and tender could be superbly unyielding and
inflexible. The gentle Savior was splendidly intolerant, and because
of His intolerance He died.

We trace the intolerance of Christ, for instance, in His attitude
toward hypocrisy. One thing that was unendurable to Jesus was the
sounding and hollow profession of religion. You can always detect
an element of pity when Jesus is face to face with other sins. There
is the yearning of infinite love over the lost—the hand outstretched
to welcome back the prodigal. But for the hypocrite there is no
gleam of pity, only the blasting and withering of wrath. "Woe unto
you, scribes and Pharisees, hypocrites." It is the intolerance of Jesus
Christ.

We trace it again in those stupendous claims that Jesus Christ put
forward for Himself. The Lord our God is a jealous God, and the

---

4. There are some fine remarks on the intolerance of the prophets in De
Quincey's paper on the Essenes, *Works*, (1890), 8:192–3. On the intolerance of
the apostles, see Denney, *Death of Christ*, pp. 110–11. James Denney (1856–
1917), Scottish Free Church theologian.

Lord our Savior is a jealous Savior. "I am the way, I am the truth, I am the life"—"No man cometh unto the Father but by Me"—"No man knoweth the Father save the Son, and He to whomsoever the Son will reveal Him." What do you make of these amazing claims and of that splendid intolerance of any rival?—yet all these words are in the Gospel-record as surely as "a bruised reed He will not break." Do you say there are many doorways to the Father? Christ Jesus stands and says, "I am the door." Do you say there are many shepherds of the sheep? Christ stands in His majesty and says, "I am the shepherd." Pitiful, merciful, full of a great compassion, Christ is intolerant of any rival; He stands alone to be worshiped and adored, or He disappears into the mists of fable. So far as I am aware, that is unique; there is nothing like it in religious history. The ancient pantheons had always room for the introduction of another god. It is Christ alone, the meek and lowly Savior, who lifts Himself up in isolated splendor. Friend of the friendless and brother of the weakest, He is intolerant of any sharing of His claims.

Again I trace this same intolerance in the allegiance which Christ demands from us. He is willing to take the lowest place upon the cross, but He will *not* take it in your heart and mine. When He was born in the fullness of the time, He did not ask for the splendor of the palace. He was born in a manger, reared in a lowly home, and grew to His manhood in obscurest station. But the moment He enters the kingdom of the heart, where He is king by conquest and by right, there everything is changed, and with a great intolerance He refuses every place except the first. "Whoso loveth father or mother more than Me is not worthy of Me"—"Let the dead bury their dead; follow thou Me." That is the word of a King in His own kingdom, claiming His rightful place among His subjects. And when you speak of the meek and lowly Jesus, never forget there is that imperial note there. He is divinely intolerant of everybody who would usurp the throne that is His right.

Such, then, are one or two instances of the intolerance of Jesus Christ, and now I want to examine its true nature that we may see how worthy it was of Christ.

The first thing I note in the intolerance of Jesus is that it is the child of glowing faith. The intolerance of Christ is little else than the other side of His perfect trust in God. When one is a stranger to you, bound by no ties of love, you are little affected by what is said about him. The talk may be true, or it may not be true, but it is none of your business, and you do not know. But the moment a man

becomes a hero to you, that moment you grow intolerant of liberties. If you believe in a woman, your heart is aflame with anger
should anyone sully her name even with a breath. A French poet
tells us that when he was a youth he was a passionate worshiper of
Victor Hugo[5]. He believed in Hugo with all his heart and soul; he
thought there had never been a poet like him. And he says that even
in a dark cellar underground, where nobody possibly could have
overheard him, he could not bear to whisper to himself that a single
verse of Hugo's poetry was bad. That is the fine intolerance of faith
in ardent and eager and devoted natures. That is the faith which
Jesus Christ was filled with, in God and His righteousness and
providential order. And with a faith like that there can be no compromise, no light and shallow acceptance of alternatives; under the
sway of such a glowing trust a certain intolerance is quite inevitable.
It is easy to be infinitely tolerant, if all that Christ lived for means
but little to you. An age that can tolerate every kind of creed is
always an age whose faith is burning low. And just because Christ's
faith burned with a perfect light and flashed its radiance full on the
heart of God, you find in Him, in all His Godward life, a steady and
magnificent intolerance.

   Then once again the intolerance of Jesus is the intolerance of
perfect understanding. It was because He knew so fully and
sympathized so deeply that there were certain things He could not
bear. One great complaint we make against intolerance is that it
does not sympathetically understand us. It is harsh in judgment and
fails in comprehension and has no conception of what things mean
for us. We have all met with intolerance like that, but remember
there is another kind. Take the case of drunkenness, for instance;
there are many people very tolerant of drunkenness. They talk about
it lightly, make a jest of it; they are none of your rigid, long-faced
Pharisees. But sometimes you meet a man, sometimes a woman, to
whom such jesting talk is quite intolerable, and it is intolerable not
because they know so little; it is intolerable because they know so
much. The curse has crossed the threshold of their home and laid its
fell grip on someone who was dear. They have seen the wreck and
ruin of it and all its daily misery and the drying up of every well-
spring of the heart. So in their grief they grow terribly intolerant,
and it is not because they do not understand; they are intolerant
because they understand so well. Never forget that it is so with

---

5. Victor Hugo (1802–1885), French poet, novelist, and dramatist.

Christ. He is intolerant because He comprehends. He knows what sin is; He knows how sweet it is; He knows its havoc, its loneliness, its dust and ashes. And therefore is He stern, uncompromising, and says to us, "Choose ye whom ye will serve." There are men who are intolerant because of ignorance; Christ is intolerant because He knows.

Lastly, the intolerance of Jesus is very signally the intolerance of love. Love bears all things—all things except one, and that is the harm or hurt of the beloved. Here is a little child out in the streets, ragged and shoeless in the raw March weather. Let it stay out until midnight, no one complains at home. Let it use the foulest of language, no one corrects it. Poor little waif, in whom all things are tolerated, and tolerated just because no one loves it! What kind of mother has that little child? What kind of father has that little child? You know them in the street, swollen and coarse, reeking with all the vileness of the city. They tolerate everything because they do not love; when love steps in that toleration ceases. Now we all know that when our Savior came, He came at the bidding and in the power of love; love wonderful, love that endured the worst, love that went up to Calvary to die. And just because that love was so intense and burned with the ardor of the heart of God, things that had been tolerable once were found to be intolerable now. That is the secret of the gospel's sternness and of its passionate protest against sin. That is why age after age it clears the issues and says, "He that is not with Me is against Me." The love that bears all things cannot bear that hurt or harm should rest on the beloved. Christ is intolerant because He loves.

And the angel said unto him, Gird thyself
and bind on thy sandals. And so he did
(Acts 12:8).

22

The Angel and the Sandals

There is a vividness of detail about this story which assures us
that facts are being recorded. No imagination, however lively, could
have conceived the scene that is presented here. When a man has
played a part in some great hour, or been an eyewitness of some
memorable action, there is a note in his telling of it, no matter how
he blunders, which is better than all the periods of historians. And
unless we be blinded by a foolish prejudice, which deadens the
literary as well as other faculties, we cannot but distinguish that
note here. Peter had been in prison once before, and once before he
had escaped miraculously. Now, having in their hands again this
prison-breaker, the authorities were determined there should be no
more miracles. But when prayer arises like a continual incense, and
when God puts out His mighty arm to help, "stone walls do not a
prison make, nor iron bars a cage."[1] Behold, the angel of the Lord
came upon Peter, and a light shined in the darkness of the prison.
And he smote Peter on the side and raised him up; and the chains
fell off from his hands and he was free. Then dazed with the sudden

---

1. From "To Lucasta, Going Beyond the Seas," Richard Lovelace (1618–
1658), English poet.

light as Peter was, thinking he dreamed and that his dream was idle, the angel said to him, "Gird thyself, and bind on thy sandals."

It is on these words I want to speak tonight, for they are rich in spiritual suggestion, and in the first place they are the angel's argument that what had happened was actually true. Peter was fast asleep when the light shone; asleep, and it was the night before his execution. A man must have a very good conscience, or a very dead one, to be able to sleep on such a night as that. Then in a moment the cell was all resplendent, and the glory of it pierced the sleep of Peter, and he opened his eyes, and the visitant was there, and he was dazed and "dark with excessive bright."[2] Was this a dream, and waking would be vain?—"Peter, bind on thy sandals, gird thyself. Art thou in doubt as to whether it is real? Employ the light I bring to tie thy shoe-latchet. Do not seek to handle me; do not inquire my name. Do not wait there wondering if it is all a dream. Gird up thy mantle and bind thy sandals on; and thou wilt speedily discover all is true." I do not think that Peter, however long he lived, would ever forget that lesson of the angel. Every morning as he stooped to tie his sandals he would say, "Even this may be an argument for liberty." Not by remarkable and striking proofs, nor by the doing of anything uncommon, not in such ways was Peter made to feel that all that had happened to him was reality. It was by doing an ordinary deed—girding his cloak and putting on his shoe—but doing it now in the light the angel brought, a light that "never was on land or sea."[3]

Now I think that that angel-argument with Peter is one that ought to be powerful with us all. There is no such proof that the new light is real as just the use of it for common deeds. We are all tempted to put things to the test in ways that are remarkable and striking. We want to say to the puddle "Be thou dry," as Bunyan did in his untutored youth. But the voice of the angel says to us, "Not so; but buckle thy mantle and bind thy sandals on, and prove in the quiet actions of today that the vision which shone on thee was not a dream." It may be a mighty proof of a man's patriotism that he is willing to drain his veins for his dear country; but to fight for that country's welfare day by day, in the face of abuse and slander, is a greater. It may be a mighty argument for love that one would lay himself down and die for Annie Laurie; but to be courteous and

---

2. From "Paradise Lost" by Milton.
3. From "Elegiac Stanzas" (1807) by Wordsworth.

kind to Annie Laurie daily is the kind of argument that all the angels love.[4] Do you seek great things for yourself? Seek them not. Use the light to tie the sandal on. Be a better father among your growing children. Be a better sister to your provoking brothers. I think that Peter would always have such thoughts when he recalled all that had happened in the prison.

Then once again our text suggests what I might call the divine economy of power. "Gird thyself, do not expect me to do it; what thou *canst* do for thyself, that thou must do." It was not pride that kept the angel from that service. Things we would scorn to do are done by angels gladly. If it was not beneath Christ to wash the feet of Peter, it was not beneath an angel to tie his shoe-latchet. But the angel refrained (as angels always do), in that economy of strength which is divine, from doing for Peter in his hour of need what it was in his power to do himself. Let Peter strive all night, he cannot loose his chains, and therefore it is the angel who does that. No beating of Peter's hands will burst the gate, and therefore it is the angel who unbars it. But "gird thyself, and bind thy sandals on"— even when God is at work there is something you can do; and that *something*, which is within your compass, will never be performed by heavenly visitant.

We see this same economy of power when we study the miracles of Jesus Christ. It is an added evidence for Jesus' miracles that the miraculous is kept down to the lowest point. He makes the wine but will not fetch the water; it is in the power of the servants to do that. He feeds the famishing thousands on the hill, but the disciples must bring the bread and distribute it. The hand of man must roll away the stone when Lazarus is to be summoned from the grave, and when the breath of life has been bestowed, it is for others to unwrap his cerements.[5]

Do you see the meaning of that divine procedure? It makes us fellow-workers with the Highest. Peter needed the angel for his rescue, but for the rescue the angel needed Peter. "Gird thyself and bind thy sandals on; do the little thou *canst* do to help me"—so Peter was lifted out of mere passivity and made a fellow-laborer

---

4. I refer of course to the refrain of the exquisite and anonymous song, "Annie Laurie"—

   And for bonnie Annie Laurie

   I'd lay me down and dee.

5. grave clothes

with God. I think of this text when I see the harvest-field, where men are busy amid the golden grain. The ministry of God has given the harvest, and now the ministry of man must bring it home. I think of it when I see men struggling heavenward, wrestling toward heaven "'gainst storm and wind and tide." It is God who has wrought in them to do His will, and now they must work out their own salvation. Do we not sometimes wonder why it should be so hard to win the crown which God delights to give? Redeemed by blood, why should we have to fight so, why struggle in deadly fashion to the end? And the answer is that thus we are ennobled and called into fellowship with the divine and raised to be sharers in that work of grace which rests on the satisfaction of Christ Jesus. All that you cannot do, God will do. All that you can do, God will never do. Trust Him to free you by bursting iron doors and leading you triumphantly from prison. But gird thyself; do not ask God to do it. Do not wait for the angel to tie on the sandal. It is only a fool who would be idle because he was assured the light had come.

Lastly, the text suggests to me a certain leisureliness in God's procedure. The angels are always bent upon their ministry, but we never find an angel in a hurry. We know the kind of man that Peter was, and how ardent and impulsive was his nature. He was always swift to speak and swift to act, too often without any reckoning of consequence. But had the calmest and most phlegmatic spirit been the tenant of that apostle's breast, it might well have been stirred into feverish haste that morning. Every moment was precious, and every moment perilous. Another instant and the soldiers might awake. Alive to his danger and to his opportunity, can you wonder if Peter clean forgot his sandals? And then the angel, calm amid that tumult, with a calmness born of fellowship with God, said "Gird thyself and put thy sandals on." I wonder if the girdle was ever so rebellious as on that morning in the prison-house. I wonder if his sandals were ever so refractory as when every moment meant life or death to Peter; but there was something imperious about this angel, and Peter had no choice but to obey. It seemed an age to Peter while he stooped, in his great agony of apprehension. What mattered the securing of his cloak when every moment was infinitely precious? But when Peter came to look back upon it all, he would see the meaning of the angel's conduct and learn the lesson (which is so hard to learn) that there is no hurry in the plans of God.

Are there not twelve hours in the day?
(John 11:9).

23

The Number of the Hours

These words were spoken by Jesus at the time when news had been brought Him that Lazarus was sick. For two days Jesus had made no move but had abode with His disciples where He was. The disciples would be certain to misconstrue that inactivity—they would whisper "Our Master at last is growing prudent"—and therefore their amazement and dismay when Christ announced He was going to Judea. They broke out upon Him with expostulation—"Lord, it was but yesterday that you were stoned there. It is as much as your life is worth to think of going—it were the rankest folly to run that tremendous risk." And it was then that Jesus turned upon the twelve, with a look which they never would forget, and said to them, "Are there not twelve hours in the day?" It is on these words that I wish to dwell a little in the quiet of this communion evening. I want to use them as a lamp to illumine some of the characteristics of the Lord. For they seem to me to irradiate first, the earnestness; second, the fearlessness; and third, the fretlessness of our Savior, Jesus Christ. First, then, their light on the earnestness of Christ.

What first arrests us, reading the life of Jesus, is not His strong intensity of purpose. It is only gradually, and as our study deepens, that we feel the push of that unswerving will. If you put the Gospel story into the hand of a pagan, to whom it came with the freshness of discovery, what would impress him would not be Christ's tenacity, but the variety and the freedom of His life. Never was there a career that bore so little trace of being lived in accordance with a plan. Never were deeds so happily spontaneous; never were words so sweetly incidental. To every moment was perfect adaptation, as if that were the only moment of existence. This hiding of intensity is mirrored in the great paintings of the face of Christ. In the galleries of the old masters I do not know one picture where the face of Christ is a determined face. For the artists felt with that poetic feeling which wins nearer to the heart of things than argument, that the earnestness of Jesus lay too deep to be portrayed by brush upon the canvas.

But when we reach the inner life of Christ, there passes a wonderful change over our thought. We slowly awake, amid all the spontaneity, to one tremendous and increasing purpose. As underneath the screaming of the seabirds we hear the ceaseless breakers on the shore, as through the rack and drift of driving clouds we catch the radiance of one unchanging star, so gradually, back of all stir and change and the varied and free activity of Christ, we discern the pressure of a mighty purpose moving without a swerve toward its goal. From the hour of His boyhood when He said to Mary, "Wist ye not that I must be about My Father's business," on to the hour of triumph on the cross when He cried with a loud voice, "It is finished," unhasting and unresting, without one check or falter, the face of Jesus is set in one direction; and it is when we come to recognize that unity, hidden amid the luxuriance of freedom, that we wake to the sublime earnestness of Christ. I think that the apostles hardly recognized it until He set His face steadfastly toward Jerusalem. Before that, they were always offering suggestions: after that, they offered them no more. They were amazed, we read; they were afraid. The eagerness of Jesus overwhelmed them. At last they knew His majesty of will and were awestruck at the earnestness of Christ.

For that wholehearted zeal were many reasons which it does not fall to me to touch on here. But one was the certain knowledge of the Lord that there were only twelve hours in His day. Before His birth, in His preexistent life, there had been no rising or setting of the sun. After His death, in the life beyond the grave, the day would be endless, for "there is no night there." But here on earth, with a mighty work to do and to get finished before His side was pierced, Christ was aroused into triumphant energy by the thought of the determined time. "I must work the works of My Father while it is day. The night cometh when no man can work." That *must*—what is it but the shadow of sunset and the breath of the twilight that was soon to fall? A day at its longest—what a little space! Twelve hours—they are ringing to evensong already! Under that power the tide, that seemed asleep, moved on "too full for sound or foam."

It is always very wonderful to me that Christ thus felt the shortness of the time. This child of eternity heard with quickened ear the muffled summons of the fleeting hours. It is only occasionally that *we* hearken to it; far more commonly we seek to silence it. Most men, as Professor Lecky says,[1] are afraid to look time in the face. But Christ was never afraid to look time in the face steadily. He eyed the sinking sands, until moved to His depths by the urgency of days, the zeal of the house of His Father ate Him up. Have you awakened to that compelling thought, or do you live as if your sun would never set? My brother, there are but twelve hours in the day, and it will be sunset before you dream of it. Get done what God has sent you here to do. Wait not for the fool's phantom of tomorrow—

> Act—act in the living Present!—
> Heart within, and God o'erhead![2]

In the next place, our text illuminates Christ's fearlessness, and that indeed is the textual meaning of it, for it was when the disciples were trying to alarm Him that Jesus silenced their suggestions so. "Master," they said, "you ought to have a care—it is a dangerous thing to show yourself at Bethany. Remember how you were stoned on your last visit; it will be almost certain death to go thither again." And it was then, to silence all their terror and with a courage as sublime as it was simple, that Jesus asked, "Are there not twelve hours in the day?" What did He mean? He meant, "I have my day. Its dawn and its sunset have been fixed by God. Nothing can shorten it and nothing can prolong it. Until the curfew of God rings out, I cannot die." It was that steadying sense of the divine disposal which made the Christ so absolutely fearless and braced Him for every "clenched antagonism" that rose with menace upon the path of duty. When Dr. Livingstone[3] was in the heart of Africa, he wrote a memo-

---

1. In the suggestive chapter on "Time," in the *Map of Life*. William Lecky (1838–1903), British historian.

2. From "Resignation" by Henry Wadsworth Longfellow (1807–1882), American poet.

3. David Livingstone (1813–1873), Scottish missionary and explorer in Africa.

rable sentence in his diary. He was ill and far away from any friend, and he was deserted by his medicine-carrier. But he was willing to go anywhere provided it was forward, and what he traced with a trembling hand was this: "I am immortal until my work is done." That was the faith of Paul and of Martin Luther, the faith of Oliver Cromwell[4] and of Livingstone. They had caught the fearless spirit of the Master who knew there were twelve hours in the day.

Now it is always a source of buoyant strength when a man comes to see that his *way* is ordered. There is a quiet courage that is unmistakable in one who is certain he is led by God. But remember, according to the Master's doctrine, our times are fixed as surely as our ways; and if we are here with a certain work to do, which in the purposes of God must be fulfilled, no harm can touch us, nor is there power in death, until it draws to sunset and to evening star. What is it that makes the Turk such a brave soldier that with all his vices we cannot but admire him? It is his conviction of a relentless fate which he cannot hasten yet cannot hope to shun. In the name of freedom, Christ rejects that fatalism; but on the ruins of it He erects another. It is the fatalism of a love that is divine, for it includes the end in the beginning. Never shirk dangers on the path of duty. On the path of duty one is always safest. Let a man be careful that he does his task, and God will take care of the task-doing man. For always there are twelve hours in the day, and though the clouds should darken into storm, they cannot hasten the appointed time when the stars come out to tell that it is night.

And just here we ought to bear in mind that the true measurement of life is not duration. We live in deeds, not breaths—it is not time, it is intensity that is life's measurement. Twelve hours of joy, what a brief space they are! Twelve hours of pain, what an eternity! We take the equal hours which the clock gives, and we mold them in the matrix of our hearts. Was it the dawn that crimsoned in the east as Romeo stood with Juliet at the window? It seemed but a moment since the casement opened, and—"It is my lady, O it is my love." But to the sufferer tossing on her sickbed and hearing every hour athwart the dark, that night went wearily with feet of lead, and it seemed as if the dawn would never break. "Are there not twelve hours in the day?" said Jesus—yet Jesus died when He was thirty-three. The dial of God has got no minute hands; its hours are

---

4. Oliver Cromwell (1599–1658), Puritan statesman, Lord Protector of England 1653–1658.

measured by service and by sacrifice. Call no life fragmentary. Call it not incomplete. Think thee how love abbreviates the hours. If God be love, time may be fiery-footed, and the goal be won far earlier than we dream.

Then lastly, and in a word or two, our text illuminates Christ's fretlessness. For never was there a life of such untiring labor that breathed such a spirit of unruffled calm. We talk about our busy modern city, and many of us *are* busy in the city, but for a life of interruption and distraction, give me the life of Jesus Christ of Nazareth. Some of us could hardly live without the hills—a day in their solitude is benediction; but when Jesus retired to that fellowship of lonely places, even there He was pressed and harassed by the crowd. Every day was thronged with incident or danger. There was no leisure so much as to eat. Now He was teaching—now He was healing—now He was parrying some cruel attack. Yet through it all, with all its stir and movement, there is a brooding calm upon the heart of Christ that is only comparable to a waveless sea asleep in the stillness of a summer evening. Some men are calm because they do not feel. We call it quiet, and it is callousness. But Christ being sinless was infinitely sensitive—quick to respond to every touch and token.

Yet He talked without contradiction of His peace—"My peace that the world cannot give or take away"—and down in the depths of that unfathomed peace was the thought of the twelve hours in the day. Christ knew that if God had given Him a twelve hours' work, God would give Him the twelve hours to do it in. To every task its time and to every time its task, *that* was one great method of the Master. And no man will ever be calm as Christ was calm who cannot halt in the midst of the stir and say, "My peace"; who cannot stop for a moment in the busiest whirl and say to himself, "My times are in Thy hand." God never blesses unnecessary labor. That is the labor of the thirteenth hour. All that God calls us to and all that love demands is fitted with perfect wisdom to the twelve. Therefore be restful; do not be nervous and fussy; leave a little leisure for smiling and for sleep. There is no time to squander, but there is time enough—are there not twelve hours in the day?

When he came to himself (Luke 15:17).

24

Coming to Oneself

In a few graphic touches Jesus delineates the kind of life the prodigal had been leading. With characteristic delicacy He does not give details. He leaves it for the elder brother to do that. We have the picture of a young man wasting his time and money—and what is worse than that, wasting his life—and like most young men who think to live that way, finding plenty of both sexes to convoy him. He is self-willed, self-indulgent, riotous—and we are just on the point of calling him contemptible. We are just on the point of thinking how to one like Jesus the prodigal must be infinitely loathsome. When suddenly a single phrase arrests us and opens a lattice into the mind of Christ and makes us suspend judgment on the prodigal. "When he came to himself"—when he became himself—then in his years of riot he was not himself. It was not the prodigal who was the real man. The real man was the penitent, not the prodigal. He was never himself until his heart was breaking, and the memories of home came welling over him until he cried, "I will arise and go to my father, and say unto him, Father, I have sinned."

I may note in passing how we have caught that tone in the kindly allowances we often make. This parable has not only influenced thought; like all the parables it has also affected language. When some one whom we love is cross or irritable, we say of him, "He's not himself today." When one whom we have known for years does something unworthy, we say, "Ah, that's not himself at all." And what is that but our instinctive certainty that a man is more than his vices or his failures, and that if you want to know him as he is, you must take him at the level of his best. It was always thus that Jesus judged humanity. He was a magnificent and a consistent optimist. He never made light of sin, never condoned it. To Him it was always terrible and tragic. But then the sinner was not the real man; sin was a bondage, a tyranny, a madness; and it was when the tyranny of sin was broken that a man came to his true self.

I would remark, too, about this prodigal that his one object in leaving home was just to find himself. When he went away into the far country, he imagined he was coming to his own. Life was intolerable on that lonely farm. There was no scope there for a young fellow's energy. And why should he be eating out his heart when the thousand voices of the world were calling him? And youth was short, and he must have his day; and he wanted to go and sound life to the deeps. So in the golden morning of desire he went away to the far country. It was impossible to realize himself at home. He would realize himself now and with a vengeance. He would live to the finest fiber of his being and come to his own in the whole range of manhood. And then, with the exquisite irony of truth, Christ shows him beggared and broken and despairing and tells us that only then, when he was dead, did he come to his true self. It is not along the path of self-willed license that a man ever reaches his best and deepest self. To be determined at all costs to enjoy is the most tragical of all mistakes. We come to ourselves when we deny ourselves, when life has room for sacrifice and service, when the eyes are lifted to the love of heaven, and the heart is set upon the will of God.

That our text was no chance expression of the Master's we may gather from many gospel passages. Think for example of that memorable hour when Jesus was journeying to Jerusalem. Our Lord had begun to speak plainly of His death, drawing the veil from the agony of Calvary; and it was all so shocking and terrible to Peter that Peter had taken Christ to task for it. "Far be it from thee, Lord; this never shall befall Thee. While I have a sword to draw they shall not touch Thee." And then the Lord flashed round on His disciple and said to him, "Get thee behind me, Satan." Only an hour before he had been Peter—"Thou art Peter, and on this rock I build." *That* was the true Peter, moved of God, kindled into the rapture of confession. But this was not Peter, though it was Peter's voice. It was something lesser and lower than the rock. Possessed by a spirit unworthy of his highest—"Get thee behind Me, Satan." In other words, Peter was not himself then, any more than the rioting prodigal was himself. There were heights in him that no one saw but Christ. There were depths in him that none but Christ had fathomed. And the glory of Christ is that in these heights and depths, and not in the meaner things that were so visible, He found the real nature of the man on whose confession the church was to be founded. It is easy to measure Peter by his fall. It is easy to measure any man by failure. Vices are more visible than virtues and form a ready-reckoner of character. But not by their worst does Jesus measure men, not by their lowest and their basest elements. Through fall and sin and denial, "Thou art *Peter*"—until at last he was Peter in very deed.

Of course in such a hopeful, splendid outlook there is no lessening of responsibility. A man is not less guilty for his failures, because they do not represent his real manhood. I have seen children playing with one another, and one would slap the other and say, "I never touched you." And when the other said, "You did, I saw you," the reply was, "It wasn't me, it was my hand." There is not a little in the maturer world of that ungrammatical and infant Jesuistry. It is so easy to make excuses for ourselves and to say, "We were ill—we were worried—it was not really me." But perhaps in all the circle of bad habits, there is no habit more fatally pernicious than the habit of making excuses for ourselves. We should always have excuses for our neighbors. We should never have excuses for ourselves. To palliate and condone our own defections is the sure way to rot the moral fiber. A man should make allowances for everybody, for we know not what is the secret story; but heaven help the man and help his character, when he begins to make allowance for himself. You will note that the prodigal made no excuses. He never said, "Young men must be young men." He never said, "My passions are my heritage, and you must make some allowance for warm blood." What He did say was, "Father, I have sinned—I have been a selfish and good-for-nothing reprobate"; and it was *then*, when his worst was in his own eyes, that his best was in the eyes of Christ. In spite of His wonderful sympathy and pity, there is a note of intense severity in Christ—"If thy right hand offend thee, cut it off. If thy right eye offend thee, pluck it out"—and in every life that is inspired by Christ there must be the echo of that same severity, urging itself not against any brother, but against the wickedness on its own bosom. I never find Jesus making any allowance for the man who makes allowance for himself. Just in proportion as you are stern with self will the Redeemer be merciful with you. Not through the meadows of easy self-excuse, but down by the very margin of despair, does a man come, as came the prodigal, to the reach and the reality of manhood.

I would further remark that when He was on earth that was one great aim of Jesus' toil. It was not to make men and women angels. It was to make men and women their true selves. They could do nothing without faith in Him, and therefore He was at all pains to quicken that; but away at the back of their dawning faith in Him was His magnificent and matchless faith in them. "Ye are the light of the world; ye are the salt of the earth"—did you ever hear such wild exaggeration? All this for a little company of rustics, provincial, unlettered, undistinguished? Ah yes, but under the warmth of such a faith in them these natures were so to grow and so to ripen that every syllable of that audacity was to prove itself literally true. The boys at Rugby used to say of Dr. Arnold,[1] "It would be mean to tell him a lie, he trusts us so." All that was best in them began to germinate under the influence of Dr. Arnold's faith. And if it was so under the trust of Arnold, what must have been the influence of Christ, when a man felt that he was trusted by those eyes that saw into the depths. Christ aimed at more than making people better; His aim and object was to make them *themselves*. He saw from the first hour all that was hidden in Simon and Matthew, Lazarus and Mary. And then He lived with them and showed what He expected and hoped undauntedly and never wearied, until at last, just like the prodigal, they came to their true selves. It took far more than their faith in Christ to do that. It took the superb faith of Christ in them. The sheep was still a sheep though in the desert. The son was still a son although a prodigal. And it was this—this faith of Christ in men—that drew them to their highest and their best, as a flower is drawn into its perfect beauty by the gentle influence of the summer sun.

And that is the reason why the follower of Christ is the possessor of the largest freedom. The nearer a man is to being himself, the nearer is he to sweet liberty. We go into certain companies, for instance, and we speedily feel that we are not at home there. What

---

1. Thomas Arnold (1795–1842), English clergyman, educator, historian, and writer.

is the word we use to express that? We say we are constrained—
that is, imprisoned. But by our own fireside and among those who
love us, we are not constrained, we have a perfect liberty; and at the
basis of that social liberty there lies the fact that there we are ourselves. It is the same in the deeper world of morals. When we are
ourselves, then are we free. It is *not* freedom to do just as we please
in defiance of all the laws that girdle us. Freedom is power to
realize ourselves, to move unfalteringly toward the vision; and the
paradox of Christianity is this, that that comes through obedience to
Christ. Think of the schoolgirl practicing her music. Is not that the
weariest of bondage? Is this the happy face we saw so lately, flushed
with the eager merriment of play? But set down the musical genius
at the instrument and get him to interpret some great master, and the
thoughts which he utters are the master's thoughts, and yet he is
magnificently free. The child is in bondage, the genius is at liberty.
The child is unnatural, the genius is himself. The child is slaving
under an outward law. The genius has the spirit of the master. And
"if any man have not the spirit of Christ," then, says the Scripture,
"he is none of His." "When he came to himself"—my brother and
my sister, the pathway to that is coming to the Savior. Jesus be-
lieves in you and in your future and in a best that is higher than your
dreams. Respond to that splendid confidence tonight. This very
hour say, "I will arise." The past is disgraceful; but the past is done
with. Thank God, there will be a different tomorrow.

And they laughed Him to scorn
(Luke 8:53).

25

The Weapon of Ridicule

This incident occurred in Capernaum, whither our Savior had just
returned. He had scarce landed when the ruler of the synagogue
besought Him that He would come and heal his daughter. Then had
occurred the interruption in the crowded street, and we can picture
the father's agony at the delay, an agony that would dull down into
despair when word came that the little maid was dead. So Jesus
entered the house with Peter and James and John. It was very
crowded and noisy and disgusting. "Weep not," He said, "the maid
is not dead, but sleepeth." Were it not better to be quiet when a tired
one sleeps? And it was then, not catching what Christ meant, nor
guessing that He spoke of a sleep that here has no awakening, that
they laughed Him to scorn, knowing that she was dead. One moment there was nothing heard but wailing, and the next the shrill
lament was drowned in laughter. One moment there was wild beating of the breast, and the next the heaping of ridicule on Christ; and
it is of ridicule, in some of its aspects and suggestions, that I wish to
speak for a moment or two tonight.

Now the first thing which I want you to observe is how often
Jesus was assailed with ridicule. Our Lord had to suffer more than
bitter hatred. He had to suffer the sneering of contempt. When a

man is *loved*, his nature expands and ripens as does a flower under the genial sunshine. When a man is *hated*, that very hate may brace him as the wind out of the north braces the pine. But when a man is *ridiculed*, only the grace of heaven can keep him courteous and reverent and tender; and Jesus Christ was ridiculed continually. "Is not this the carpenter's Son; do we not know His brothers?" "He is the friend of publicans and sinners." Men ridiculed His origin. Men ridiculed His actions. Men ridiculed His claims to be Messiah. Nor in all history is there such exposure of the cruelty and bestiality of ridicule as in the mocking and taunting at the cross, with its purple robe and its reed and crown of thorns. Think of that moment when, all forspent and bleeding, Jesus was brought out before the people; and Pilate cried to them, "Behold your king! Is not this broken dreamer like a Caesar?" That was the cruel ridicule of Rome, often to be repeated by her satirists, and it was all part of the cross which Jesus bore. It is not enough to say that Christ was hated, if you would sound the deeps of His humiliation. There is something worse for a true man than being hated, and that something worse is being scorned; and we must never forget that in the cup, which Christ prayed in Gethsemane might pass from Him, there was this bitter ingredient of scorn.

Nor should we think that because Christ was Christ He was therefore impervious to ridicule. On the contrary, just because Christ was Christ He was most keenly susceptible to its assault. It is not the coarsest but the finest natures that are most exposed to the wounding of such weapons, and in the most sensitive and tender heart scorn, like calumny, inflicts the sorest pain. When Lord Byron[1] published his first little book of poems, and when he was covered with ridicule by the Scotch reviewers for it, he was stung into an act of swift retaliation, but there is no trace that he felt that derision deeply. But when Keats,[2] casting *his* poems on the world, met with like treatment from the same reviewers, it almost, if not quite, broke his heart. Both were true poets, touched by the sacred fire, but the one was of finer fiber than the other, and it was he of the sensitive and tender heart who was likely to be broken by the pitiless storm. Now think of Christ, uncoarsened by transgression, exquisite in all faculty and feeling, and you will understand how, to a soul like His, it was so bitter to be laughed to scorn. I thank God

---

1. George Gordon (Lord) Bryon (1788–1824), English poet.
2. John Keats (1795–1821), English poet.

that the Savior of the world had not the steeled heart of a Roman Stoic.[3] I thank God He was so rich in sympathy and so perfectly compassionate and tender. But I feel that the other aspect of that beauty must have been exquisite susceptibility to pain, and not alone the pain of spear and nail, but the more cruel and deep-searching pain of ridicule.

Probably it is thus we may explain why ridicule is most keenly felt when we are young. It is not at sixty, it is at one-and-twenty, that we are most afraid of being ridiculous. "He was one of those sarcastic young fellows," says Thackeray of young Pendennis,[4] "that did not bear a laugh at his own expense, and of all things in the world feared ridicule most"; and Sir Walter Scott, speaking of the enthusiasms of his own boyhood, said, "At that time I feared ridicule more than I have ever done since."[5] There are many young men who could bear to be thought wicked, but I never met one who could bear to be thought ridiculous; indeed I have found them doing ridiculous things just to escape the taint of being thought so; and my point is that that temptation—for it is such—falls at its fiercest on the heart of youth, because in youth we are sensitive and eager and not yet hardened by traffic with the world.

It is notable, too, that Christ was laughed to scorn because the people failed to understand Him. It was because they had not caught His meaning that they burst thus into derisive laughter. "The maiden," said Jesus, "is not dead but sleeping"; and they were without imagination, and they took it literally. They had no heart for that mystic and poetic speech that calls the last closing of the eyes a sleep. "Our friend Lazarus sleepeth," He said once, "but I go to awake him out of sleep." He thought of His friend whose spirit had departed as of one who had fallen upon the peace of slumber. So here, to the noisy mourners in Capernaum, "The maiden is not dead, but sleepeth"—and they laughed Him to scorn and covered Him with ridicule; and they did it because they could not understand.

The same truth meets us in the story of Pentecost, as we read it in

---

3. School of philosophy founded by Zeno who taught that humans should be free from passion, unmoved by joy or grief, and submit without complaint to unavoidable necessity.

4. William Makepeace Thackeray (1811–1863), English novelist.

5. Lockhart, *Life*, 1. Cf. also Newman, *Parochial and Plain Sermons*, 7:4, "On the Praise of Men." Sir Walter Scott (1771–1832), Scottish novelist and poet.

the vivid narrative of Acts. There also, on the birthday of the church, we light on ridicule, and there also it is the child of ignorance. For there came a sound as of a mighty rushing wind, and the spirit of God fell on the little company, and they were exalted marvelously by the gift and went out in the glory of it to preach Christ—and the people, blind to the source of their enthusiasm, mocked at them as though they had been drunk. "These men are filled with new wine," they said. It was not an argument, it was a sneer. They could not comprehend what this might mean, but at any rate they could heap derision on it. So once again, on the page of Holy Scripture, that perfect mirror of the human heart, we have an instance of ridicule which sprang from an incapacity to understand.

I therefore trust that the young men here tonight will appraise ridicule at its true value. It is not always the token of superior cleverness. It is far oftener the mark of incapacity. Many of us remember how, not so long ago, it was the custom to ridicule the Salvation Army. In the press, on the street, and on the stage at pantomimes, the Army was held up to derision. But no one ridicules the Salvation Army now. Men may object to its methods, but they do not laugh at it. And why? because they know it better now and have learned how gallant and pure is its enthusiasm. It is the gradual increase of knowledge and of light that has made that ridicule impossible today. It has died a natural death and been replaced by admiration or by argument. And if in this case and a thousand other cases, a clearer knowledge makes ridicule ridiculous—do you not see the point I am driving at, that ridicule is the handy weapon of the ignorant? You cannot refute a sneer, said Dr. Johnson;[6] but if you cannot refute it, at least you can despise it. A sneer is the apology for argument made by a man who does not understand. And that is why, though you find Christ Jesus angry, you never find Him ridiculing anybody, for every secret of every human heart was perfectly understood by the Redeemer.

Of course I am aware that in a world like this there is a certain work for ridicule to do.[7] So long as shams and pretensions are

---

6. Samuel Johnson (1709–1784), English lexicographer, critic, and poet.

7. How far ridicule is a test of truth was a subject once keenly debated. The debate finds a place in literature in the third book of Akenside's *Pleasures of the Imagination*, a powerful, but I fear much-neglected, poem. In the Introduction to my fine old copy (Griffin & Co.: Glasgow, 1825) it is stated that Akenside took his defense of ridicule from Shaftesbury, and was attacked for it by Warburton.

abroad, a little gentle ridicule is needed. There are some things that should never be taken seriously—they are in their nature so utterly ridiculous—and against *these* things no man with any humor would ever plant the great guns of his argument. A jest is sometimes the wisest of all answers, and a little raillery the best of refutations. The world owes not a little to these ready spirits who can answer a fool according to his folly. Professor Lecky tells us[8] that in the Middle Ages the troubadours did one great service to humanity. It was a time when the minds of men were darkened by grotesque and horrible teachings about hell. No one dared argue with the medieval church—it might have cost a common man his life to argue—but the wandering troubadours in their fantastic songs poured ridicule upon these priestly horrors and by their badinage helped on a brighter day. So too in Spain in the sixteenth century, when the popular literature was the romance of chivalry, do you think that preaching could have weaned the people from those so vapid and unedifying books? But Cervantes,[9] in his superb *Don Quixote*, turned the whole literature of romance into a jest and brought men to their senses by a laugh. At a party, at which Charles Lamb[10] was present, there was a gentleman who was loud in his praises of Islam. He would have all the company convinced that Mohammed was far superior to Christ. It does not appear that Lamb discussed the matter. There is certainly not a sign that he got angry. Probably he felt himself incompetent to debate the high matters in dispute. But as the company was dispersing, the gentleman lost his hat, and when Lamb was asked if he had seen it, "I thought," said the stammering and gentle Elia, "I thought that our friend came *in a turban!*"[11] That was a stroke of the most exquisite ridicule. It was answering a fool according to his folly. You may depend upon it that it would be remembered when all the arguments were quite forgotten. And so long as the world has foolish people in it, who strain at the gnat and swallow down the camel, so long will there be an office in the world for the gentle raillery of ridicule. But remember that the ridicule of genius is very different from the sneering of the world—that mockery which the world loves to cast upon every enthusiasm and aspiration. It is not because it understands so much, it is be-

---

8. *Hist. Europ. Mor.*, 4.

9. Miguel de Cervantes (1547–1616), Spanish novelist and short story writer.

10. Charles Lamb (1775–1834), English essayist and critic.

11. See Lucas, *Life of Lamb*, 2:128.

cause it understands so little, that in Capernaum and here, it laughs to scorn.

I should like to say also to those who are tempted to see only the ridiculous side of things, that perhaps in the whole gamut of the character, there is nothing quite so dangerous as that.[12] The man who is always serious has his risks, for there is more laughter in God's works than he imagines. The man who always argues has his risks, for there are truths too fine to be meshed in any argument. But the man who ridicules what is true and high and noble had a thousand times better never have been born into a world so strangely built as this. It is so easy to raise a laugh at things. It is so cheaply and absurdly easy. And there are men whose only claim to being superior is that they are able to win that little triumph. But I call that the most degrading of all triumphs, and that not only for the harm it does to others, but far more for the irreparable harm that it surely brings upon the man himself. Life is not worth living without some high ideal. Life is quite worthless unless we live it reverently. If there be nothing above us and beyond us, we may as well give up the struggle in despair. And the strange thing is that when we take to ridiculing all that is best and worthiest in *others*, by that very habit we destroy the power of believing in what is worthiest in *ourselves*. It was not a caprice that when Jesus Christ was ridiculed, He turned the mockers out of the miracle-chamber. That is what the Almighty always does when men and women take themselves to mocking. He shuts the door on them, so that they cannot see the miracles with which the universe is teeming, and they miss the best, because in their blind folly they have laughed the Giver of the best to scorn. Therefore I beg of you never take to ridicule. If you have started the habit, give it up tonight. I beg of you also, never be turned by ridicule from what you know to be right and good and holy. You serve a Master who was laughed to scorn, but you also serve a Master who despised the shame, and the servant is not greater than his Lord.

---

12. Rev. David Smith, *Days of His Flesh*, p. 392 note, suggests that Mark and Luke substitute "colt" for the "ass" on which Christ rode, to avoid provoking ridicule among the Greeks and Romans for whom they wrote.

In the day that thou stoodest on the other
side (Obad. 11).

26

The Unconcerned Spectator

It is perhaps impossible to tell what are the precise events here
spoken of. This little book, as one has said, has been tossed from
century to century of Jewish history. All we can be certain of is that
Jerusalem had been captured; its enemies had assailed it, and it had
fallen; and in the hour of that assault Edom did nothing; it stood as
an onlooker on the other side. Edom was not a distant country—it
lay just across the Jordan to the south. Edom was not a land of
foreigners—the Edomites were the children of Esau, Jacob's brother. Yet in the day of Judah's direst need, when her enemies were
thundering at her gates, Edom was content to be an onlooker. That
is what stirs to hot anger the heart of Obadiah, as he recalls the hour
when Jerusalem was devastated. It is that a brother-nation should
never have raised a finger to help their hard-pressed brothers in
their need. So Edom is cursed for being a looker-on—for playing
no part in the drama at its gates—for assuming the attitude of
culpable neutrality.

It is to be observed, too, that this attitude is blamed because the
cause of Jerusalem is the cause of God. There was far more being
enacted across Jordan than the common onset of one tribe upon
another. The Bible does not encourage interference. It does not

incite men to rush into every quarrel. "Man, who made *Me* a judge or divider over you," was the answer of Jesus once to two disputing brothers. But this was far more than a quarrel between parties. It was a phase of the unceasing battle between light and darkness. Jerusalem was God's city—she stood for the cause of God—and it was against God that her besieging foes were fighting. Had it been a mere quarrel between two jealous states, Edom had been well advised to take no part in it. She had her fields to till, and she had her vines to cultivate; it would have been folly to have interfered. But this to the prophet was not a strife of party. It was right against wrong; it was goodness against evil; and it was because in that conflict Edom took no part, that Obadiah launched God's curse on her.

Now no one can be an attentive student of the Bible without finding that from first to last it takes that view. Where moral and spiritual issues are at stake, it regards neutrality with a divine abhorrence. "I would thou wert cold or hot," says Christ to the Laodiceans, "I would thou hadst taken a clear stand upon one side. I should have more hopes of thee if thou wert thoroughly in earnest, even if it were in the service of the adversary; but because thou art lukewarm—neither cold nor hot—because thou art a mere onlooker like Edom—what can I do but reject thee with contempt?" For always, whether in Judah or in Laodicea, the battle between earth and heaven is being waged; it takes a thousand forms, moves to a thousand issues, clothes itself in the burning questions of the hour; and in *that* battle one thing that God abhors and visits with His curse throughout the whole of Scripture is the attitude of standing aloof and looking on.

Think, for example, of the curse of Meroz, as we find it in the Book of Judges. "Curse ye Meroz," said the angel of the Lord, "curse ye bitterly the inhabitants thereof: because they came not to the help of the Lord, to the help of the Lord against the mighty." Deborah and Barak had gained a noble victory over the Canaanites under their captain Sisera. It was a gallant and hazardous attempt, and men had taken their lives into their hands to dare it. And what was Meroz? Some little highland village lying asleep in the shelter of the hills. And its men were busy toiling for their bread, and at the best it was an insignificant place. And it lay far away from the line of march of Sisera, and really it had little interest in the matter. But "Curse ye Meroz," said the angel of the Lord, "because it came not to the help of the Lord against the mighty." God will accept many an excuse for honest error; but God will accept no excuse for being neutral. So Meroz has perished—no man knows its site—it has been cast by the arm of heaven into oblivion—and all because, like Edom, in the hour of trial it stood aloof and played the looker-on.

Of course we should always bear in mind that a man may *seem* neutral without being really so. It is not always the enthusiastic advocates who do most for the cause that needs assistance. Great causes do not only need their rank and file who will go forward gallantly into the heat of combat, they need their captains too, who can stand apart a little and guide the varying fortunes of the day.

Think for example of our Savior's attitude toward such a problem as that of slavery. In a land like Palestine, which was a Roman province, He must have been face to face with slavery every day. He saw the degradation it involved. He saw the infamous cruelties it sanctioned. He saw how it trampled into the dust those rights and liberties which in His eyes belonged to every man. Yet I study the teaching of Christ from first to last, I note its rebukes and fierce denunciations, yet not one word of defiance can I find against this traffic in the lives of men. Were there no noble reformers in Judea whose hearts were all aflame at that iniquity? Did they never say, "Ah, how our cause would triumph if we had the eloquence of Jesus on our side? Cast down the gauntlet, Master, do not stand aloof; come over and help us in our battle for the slave"—yet that is just what Jesus never did. He went on His way preaching the glad tidings, healing the sick, training the twelve disciples; until the hot-hearted reformers were disgusted and said, "This Messiah is of no use to us." Has history confirmed their shallow verdict? Has Christ been neutral in that mighty battle? Is it not His spirit, working through the ages, that has made the cause victorious at last? The best and mightiest friend the slave has had has been the Prophet who was born at Nazareth; yet the zealous champions of the slave in Galilee said, "He is standing on the other side."

I therefore counsel you never to judge rashly on this question of *other* men's neutrality. Every great cause has need of a thousand advocates, and every advocate must work in his own way. It takes more than a Luther to make a Reformation, it takes the brain of an Erasmus[1] too. And a French Revolution needs more than a fiery

---

1. Desiderius Erasmus (1466?–1536), Dutch humanist, scholar, theologian and writer.

Danton;[2] it needs the musings and the dreams of a Rousseau.[3] God cannot do without His fierce enthusiasts who plunge into the thickest of the battle—they bear the burden and the heat of conflict, and they shall not be forgotten in the roll-call; but the great peril of such enthusiasts is this, to think that they alone are in the strife and to forget that in every great reform God fulfills Himself in many ways. God needs the poet who does not work by argument, but who sees as in a vision what is truth. God needs the thinker who lives remote from strife and grapples with the great problems in his solitude. God needs the dreamer with his dim apocalypse; He needs the mystic with his interior way. And He needs them, not merely for His glory, but for every battle that rages round Jerusalem. Be very chary then of judging others in this decisive matter of neutrality. They may be doing a great deal more than you, though in *your* judgment they may be doing nothing. Find your own task; give yourself wholly to it; scorn to be neutral in this world of cleavage; and then believe you have a thousand allies whom probably you shall never recognize.

Now the great evil of neutrality is this, that it puts a man hopelessly out of touch with God, and to be out of touch and harmony with God is nothing else than the high-road to death. If God be neutral to the welfare of humanity then I can be neutral and still enjoy His favor. But if God be intensely and passionately earnest that the right should conquer and the wrong be slain, then to be neutral is to disgrace that image in which I, and all the human race, were made. The Epicureans[4] of the old world, as you know, pictured the gods as utterly indifferent. They thought that they feasted and loved and lived forever in an unruffled and ungodly ease. No echo of human sorrow ever reached them. No cry of a breaking heart ever distressed them. The shouting of voices in the world's dim struggle never flecked the sunshine of elysium.[5] You cannot wonder that a neutral heaven like that fostered in the citizens of Rome a neutral character. As a man's god is, so will a man become. Give him an indifferent heaven, and he becomes indifferent. Hence

---

2. Georges Jacques Danton (1759–1794), French revolutionary leader.

3. Jean Jacques Rousseau (1712–1778), French philosopher, author, and social reformer.

4. Disciples of Epicurus (342?–270 B.C.), Greek philosophers, who taught that the highest good is pleasure.

5. The abode of the blessed after death in classical mythology.

history, with that wisdom of selection which laughs at the definitions of philosophy, looks at the self-pleasing and indifferent man and calls him to this day Epicurean.

Have you ever been tempted to that old philosophy? To think that God sleeps—upon the other side? There are few men who have not been tempted so, but in that temptation we are saved by Christ. Can a *mother* be unconcerned about the heathen when she gives her daughter to be a missionary in foul Calabar? Can a *father* be indifferent to his country when he gives the son of his love to fight and die for it? And can *God* be neutral—an unconcerned spectator in the unceasing struggle between light and darkness—when in the fullness of the time He sent to earth His only begotten Son our Savior Christ? That gift assures me that the heart in heaven is passionately interested in the drama. It tells me that whatever be the case on *earth*, within the gates of heaven there is no neutrality. And therefore I charge you, as you would hope for heaven and for fellowship with Him who sent a Savior, beware of the attitude of looking on, and come to the help of the Lord against the mighty.

Then is the offense of the cross ceased
(Gal. 5:11).

27

The Offense of the Cross

One thing which marks the ministry of Paul is how he lovingly yearned over the Jews. With a quenchless and intense desire, he prayed that they might be brought into the fold. Never did mother so long for the saving of her son as Paul longed for the saving of his countrymen. He was willing to suffer anything or everything, if only his people Israel might be won.

It is when we remember that deep longing that we realize what the Cross meant for Paul. For the great stumbling-block of faith to the Jews—the offense that made the gospel of Christ smell rank to them—was, as our text indicates, the Cross. Take that away, and it would be a thousand times more easy to win the Jews to the acceptance of the Lord. Say nothing about that, just slur it over, and you would take half the difficulty out of the way of Israel. Yet in spite of his yearning to see Israel saved, that was the one theme which Paul would not ignore. God forbid, he says, that I should glory save in the Cross of Jesus Christ my Lord. There is a great lesson there for Christian teachers and for all who are trying to advance Christ's kingdom. The more earnest and eager they are to have men saved, the more willing are they to go all lengths to meet them. And that is right, for we must be all things to all men—to the Jews as a Jew, to the Romans as a Roman; but remember there are a few great facts we cannot yield, though they run counter to the whole spirit of the age. It were better to empty a church and preach the Cross, than to fill it by keeping silence like a coward. It were better to fail as Paul failed with the Jews, than to succeed by being a traitor to the Cross. And that is why I look with such uncertainty on much that the church is trying to do today. Religion can never be a pleasant entertainment. When the offense of the Cross ceases, it is lost.

Now I want tonight to make a little plainer to you why the Cross was an offense to the Jews and to put things in such a way that you may see at once that the same causes are operative still.

First, then, the Cross was offensive to the Jews just because it blighted all their hopes. It shattered every dream they ever dreamed, every ideal that ever glimmered on them. No telegram of news full of disaster, plunging a man into unlooked-for poverty—no sudden death of one whom the heart clings to, laying a man's life in ruins at his feet—not these more certainly shatter a man's hopes than did the Cross the vision of the Jews. They had prayed for and had dreamed of their Messiah, and He was to come in power as a conqueror. "Prepare ye the way of the Lord, make His paths straight"—you can almost hear the tramp of victorious feet. *That* was the light which burned in the Jewish darkness; that was the song which made music in their hearts. Then in the place of that triumph, there comes Calvary. In place of the Christ victorious, Christ crucified. And was this the Messiah who was to trample Rome, pierced in hands and feet by Roman nails? To the Jews a stumbling-block—you cannot wonder at it, when every hope they had formed was contradicted. Yet in spite of it all, Paul preached Christ crucified, and that was the offense of the Cross.

Now I venture to say that that offense of Calvary is just as powerful now as it was then. If I know anything about the ideals men cherish now and about the hopes that are regnant in ten thousand hearts, they are as antagonistic to the Cross as was the Jewish ideal of Messiah. Written across Calvary is sacrifice; written across this age of ours is pleasure. On the lips of Christ are the stern words, I must die. On the lips of this age of ours, I must enjoy. And it is when I think of the passion to be rich and the judgment of everything by money-standards; of the feverish desire at all costs to be happy; of the frivolity, of the worship of success; it is when I think of that and then contrast it with the "pale and solemn scene" upon the hill, that I know that the offense of Calvary is not ceased. Unto the Jews a stumbling-block—unto far more than the Jews—unto a pleasure-loving world and a dead church. Therefore say nothing about it; let it be; make everything interesting, pleasant, easy. Then is the offense of the Cross ceased—and with it the power of the Gospel.

Once more, the Cross was an offense to the Jews because it swept away much that they took a pride in. If there was any meaning in Calvary at all, some of their most cherished things were valueless. The Jews were preeminently a religious people, and this is always one peril of religious people. It is to take the things that lead to God and let the heart grow centered upon them. There was the ceremonial law for instance, with its scrupulous abhorrence of defilements. No one who has not studied the whole matter can ever know what that meant to the Jew. And there were the sacrifices smoking upon their altars and the feasts and festivals and journeys to Jerusalem. And there was the Temple, that magnificent building, sign of their hope and symbol of their unity. At least let this be said of that old people, that if they were proud, they were proud of worthy things. It is better to be proud of law and temple than to be proud of battleship and millionaire. Yet all that pride, religious though it was—that pride, deep-rooted as the people's life—all that was swept away like autumn leaves if there was any meaning in the Cross. No more would the eyes of men turn to Jerusalem, no more would sacrifices fill the altars, no more was there room for ceremonial law if the Son of God had died upon the tree. And it was this crushing into the very dust of all that was dearest to the Jewish heart that was so bitter an offense of Calvary.

And today has that offense of the Cross ceased? Has that stumbling-block been removed out of the way? I say that this is still the offense of Calvary, that it cuts at the root of so much that we are proud of. Here is a woman who strives to do her duty. God bless her, she does it very bravely. Here is a student proud of his high gifts. God prosper him that he may use them well. But over against reliance upon duty and all attempts of the reason to give peace, there hangs the crucified Redeemer saying, "No man cometh unto the Father but by Me." Here is the offense of the Cross in cultured ages. It is that a man must come with empty hands. He must come as one who knows his utter need of the pardoning mercy of Almighty God; and in an age like ours, that leans upon its heritage and is proud of its magnificent achievement, that call to unconditional surrender is the offense of evangelical religion. We are all tempted to despise what we get freely. We like a little toil and sweat and travail. We measure the value of most things not by their own worth but by all that it has cost us to procure them. And Calvary costs us nothing though it cost God everything; the love and the life of it are freely offered; and to a commercial age and a commercial city there is something suspicious and offensive there. Ah sirs, if I preached salvation by good works what an appreciative audience I could have. How it would appeal to many an eager heart in the young and teeming life of this great city. But I trample that temptation under foot, not that I love you less but that I love Christ more, and I pray that here, where the gospel is proclaimed, the offense of the Cross of Christ may never cease. I do *not* believe that if you scratch a man you will find underneath his skin a Christian. I do *not* believe that if you do your best all is well for time and for eternity. But I *do* believe—

> Not the labors of my hands
> Can fulfill Thy law's demands;
> Could my zeal no respite know,
> Could my tears forever flow,
> All for sin could not atone:
> Thou must save, and Thou alone.[1]

But again, the Cross was an offense to the Jews because it obliterated national distinctions. It leveled at one blow those social barriers that were of such untold worth in Jewish eyes. It was supremely important that the Jews should stand apart; through their isolation God had educated them. They had had the bitter-sweet privilege of being lonely, and being lonely they had been ennobled. Unto them were committed the oracles of God; they were a chosen nation, a peculiar people. The covenants were theirs; theirs were the promises; the knowledge of the one true God was theirs; until at last, almost inevitably, there rose in the Jewish mind a certain separateness and a certain contempt, continually deepening, for all the other nations of mankind. They had no envy of the art of Greece. They were not awed by the majesty of Rome. Grecians and Romans, Persians and Assyrians— powerful, cultured, victorious—were but Gentiles. There is something almost sublime in the contempt with which that little nation viewed the world. Then came the Cross and leveled all distinctions—burst through all barriers of nationality. There was neither Jew nor Gentile, Greek nor barbarian, but Christ was all and in all. Let some wild savage from the farthest west come to the Cross of Christ pleading for mercy, and he

---

1. "Rock of Ages" by Augustus Toplady (1740–1778), Anglican hymnwriter.

had nothing less to do, and nothing more, than the proudest Jew who was a child of Abraham. One feels in an instant the insult of it all; how it left the Jew defenseless in the wild. All he had clung to was gone; his vineyard-wall was shattered; he must live or die now in the windswept world. And this tremendous leveling of distinctions—this striking out Jew and writing in humanity—this, to the proud, reserved, and lonely people, was no small part of the offense of Calvary.

Now I would not have you imagine for a moment that Christ disregards all personal distinctions. If I sent you away harboring the thought that all who come to Christ get the same treatment, I should have done Him an unutterable wrong. In everything He did Christ was original, because He was fresh from God into the world; but in no sphere was He so strikingly original as in the way in which He handled those who came to Him. So was it when He was on the earth; so is it now when He is hid with God. There is always some touch, some word, some discipline, that tells of an individual understanding. But in spite of all that and recognizing that, I say that this is the "scandal" of the Cross, that there every distinction is obliterated, and men must be saved as lost or not at all. You remember the lady from a gentle home who went to hear the preaching of George Whitefield?[2] And she listened in disgust to a great sermon and then, like Naaman, went away in a rage. "For it is perfectly intolerable," she said, "that ladies like *me* should be spoken to just like a creature from the streets." Quite so—it *is* perfectly intolerable— and that is the stumbling-block of Calvary. Are you, who may be cultured to your fingertips, to be classed with the savage who cannot read or write? It would be very pleasant to say No—but then were the offense of the Cross ceased. A friend of mine who is a busy doctor in a thriving borough not ten miles from Glasgow was called in the other day to see a patient who, as was plain at the first glance, was dying. And the doctor, a good Christian, said, "Friend, the best service I can do you is to ask, Have you made your peace with God?" Whereon the man, raising his wasted arm and piercing the questioner with awe-filled eyes, said, *"Doctor, is it as bad as that?"* I want to say it is always as bad as that. I want to say it to the brightest heart here. You do need pardon and peace with God in Christ as much as the wildest prodigal in Glasgow. Accept it. It is freely offered you. Say, "Thou, O Christ, art all I want." And then, just as the wilderness will blossom, so will the offense of the Cross become its glory.

---

2. George Whitefield (1714–1770), English evangelist.

And he [Moses] looked this way and that
way, and when he saw that there was no
man, he slew the Egyptian (Ex. 2:12).

28

Unobserved Sins

That this was a very rash and wicked action, none of us can have
any doubt at all. It was not thus that Moses was to prosper in
delivering his people from the yoke of Egypt. In reading the story
of African exploration I have been struck by one recurring feature.
It is how often the most successful expeditions have to tell the sorry
tale of a bad start. Well this was a bad start—this act of man-
slaughter—in the deliverance of Israel from their bondage; and
Moses had to learn that not in ways like that was it the will of God
to free His people. No doubt there was abundant provocation, and
Moses by nature had a fiery temper. The man who shattered the
tables of the law could never have been a cold and calculating
person. And if the missionaries on the Congo, when they see the
brutalities there, are moved to their very depths with indignation,
we can understand the surge of Moses' passion when he saw a
brother lashed by an Egyptian. But for all that, it was an unworthy
deed. At the best it was what Bacon calls "wild justice."[1] It is not by
sudden attacks of furious rage that nations are liberated and reforms

1. From "Of Revenge" by Francis Bacon (1561–1626), English philosopher
and essayist

accomplished. And I sometimes wonder if Moses on the Mount, when he read on the table of stone "Thou shalt not kill," remembered this wild hour when he slew the Egyptian and dug a pit in the sand to hide the corpse.

Now I do not wish to dwell on the whole incident but rather on this graphic text—"He looked this way and that way, and when he saw there was no man, he slew the Egyptian." That suggests to me two lines of thought to which I ask your attention for a little. First, to think oneself unobserved often makes way for sin; second, unobserved sin may have far-reaching consequences.

First, then, to think oneself unobserved often makes way for sin. Moses looked this way and that way, and he saw no man. That does not mean, I take it, that no one was in sight, for there would not be an Egyptian overseer over one Israelite; it means that there was no one watching; there was not an eye directed to the place. Far off, the guards were marching before the gates of Memphis. Away on the fields the Israelites were toiling. But the sun was high, and the noonday light was dazzling, and the shimmering heat had made the liveliest drowsy. Had any eye been fixed upon the spot, Moses unquestionably would have curbed his passion. One onlooker, who might have carried word to Pharaoh—and the blow that slew the Egyptian had been stayed. But there were no spectators—everyone was occupied; Moses was unwatched and unobserved; and it was the thought of being unobserved that tempted Moses to his homicide.

There is a somewhat similar scene in the New Testament in the story of the denial of Simon Peter. What made it so easy for Peter to fall that night was the thought that there was nobody to see. There are some natures which are intensely sensitive to the reproaching or upbraiding look of human eyes. It is when the principles of right and wrong are gathered into the looks of those who love them, that they feel most powerfully the summons to be good or know the bitterest agonies of shame. It is so with emotional and tenderhearted men; it was conspicuously so with Simon Peter. To withdraw from Peter the eyes of those who loved him was to leave him unconfirmed as any child. Do you think he would ever have denied his Lord if the band of his brother-disciples had been there? A word from Philip or a glance from John would have recalled him in a flash to his true self. But Peter looked this way and that way, and he saw no man—no man who knew him, no man who understood; and in the sudden assurance that he was unobserved, Peter denied his Lord.

Now ages have fled since Peter and Moses lived, yet life is still beset with the same peril. The heart in its deeper places mocks the centuries and links us all together into kinship. There are multitudes to whom the smile of heaven means little, but who would not forfeit for worlds the smile of men. There are many whom the fear of God cannot restrain who are yet restrained by the fear of human censure. And sin, taking occasion by that law, whispers to men that they are unobserved and so makes it easier to transgress.

We see it, for instance, in men who go abroad, whether to travel or to settle down. It is a matter of common notoriety how often men are different when abroad. At home they spend a quiet and restful Sunday, redeeming the time by worship and by service; but abroad they do a hundred things on Sunday that they would have been ashamed to do in Scotland. I grant you that that is not the highest type of character. In the highest character there is always a fine permanence. The man who is rooted in the life of God will show himself the same in every land. All I say is that there are men innumerable who have led orderly and cleanly lives at home, and who go to Africa and to India or to Paris and there behave themselves in very different fashion. Like Moses they look this way and that way, and they see no man. They thrill with the thought that they are unobserved. The strong restraint of a neighborhood that knows them is no longer operative in a foreign country. And just because they deem themselves unnoticed, they take unwarrantable and unworthy liberties, which they would never dream of taking when surrounded by the watchful eyes of love. That is why it is so imperative for our young men to have matters settled before they go abroad. When a man has given himself to God in faith, there is always One who sees and understands. By the lakes of Africa, in the cities of India, amid the color and music of continental towns, a man has always an audience of love when he has with him the presence of his Lord.

Again, I think we are face to face with this peril in the seclusion and secrecy of home. There are men with whose conduct the world can find no fault, but whose behavior at home is quite contemptible. Of course such men at the heart of them are cowards, but that does not in the least excuse their conduct, for the cowardice that wreaks itself upon the family-circle is perhaps the most contemptible of all. Far am I from saying that one should be at home just what he is in his converse with the world. There is a happy freedom in the home which we neither look for nor practice in society. And just because love is so exquisitely sensitive—so quick to discern the cloud on the horizon—so often homes that are most rich in love are most exposed to the falling of the shadow. But the penalties we pay for love are one thing, and the evils we lovelessly inflict another; and home may be a sphere of meanest torment, because it is so secret and secluded. Are there none here who have a smile for everybody, except for the one who longs for it at home? Are there none whom all the world would call good-natured, saving the one heart that has to live with them? Ah yes, we look this way and that way, and we see no man. We are secure from observation in our dwellings. The peril of home for a certain type of character is just the peril of being unobserved.

Once more, in our modern civilization this is one of the dangers of our cities. It is because men and women think themselves unseen there that the way of degradation is so easy. Those of you who have had your homes in country places—and there are many here tonight who have had that—know well that you can draw no sharp distinction between town and country, giving the town a monopoly of vice. It is part of the disenchantment of experience, which the wise man must live through and overcome, to find the fairest corners of God's world so tainted and so defiled with sin. Still for all that, in our great and teeming cities, there is a depth of misery, a rioting of vice; there is an excess of squalor and of evil of which the rural hamlet knows but little; and at the back of that, with many other causes, there can be no question that one cause is this, the dying out of the thought that men are known. In the village no one is a stranger. The humblest man in the village stands apart. Each one knows every one, nods to him in the street, meets him at market, sees him in the church; and it takes a man who is very bent on evil to break through all these barriers of respect. But the villager drifts into the city, and from that hour he ceases to be a unit. He is swept into the crowd of those who toil and die; he looks upon a thousand faces and knows none. Until at last, feeling his insignificance and how indifferent to all he does is mighty Babylon, it becomes harder for a man to stand and a thousand times easier to fall. In the village he looked this way and that way, and he saw some who had known him from his childhood. In the city he looks this way and that way, and he sees no man—no one who knows or cares. And could we read the tale of many a life that was cradled in Highland glen and here was wrecked, somewhere among the causes of its ruin we should find the city-born sense that there was none to see. That is the value of a little human sympathy on the part of those who go down among the lapsed. If you cannot speak to them about religion, you can at least show them that you care. And who can tell what a kindly word may do in helping a man to feel that he is known, or how it may strengthen him against these sins that grow so easy when we are unobserved.

Now in the second place, and in a word, unobserved sins may have far-reaching consequences. Moses saw no man—his sin was unobserved—yet his sin profoundly modified his future. He had to fly to Midian as the result of it, and he had to wait in Midian forty years; he was an old man with a silvered head, when God restored him to deliver Israel. What did he dream of in those desert days, when he led his sheep to pasturage and stream? What did he think of it all—spending his manhood there, and Israel still toiling in the fields of Egypt? Did he not learn that bitterest of lessons that by those sins which we imagine no man sees, the best days of our manhood may be lost, and our power for the service of God be thrown away?

I therefore urge you never to imagine that you can escape the consequence of undetected evil. Somehow or other it gets written out, so that he who has eyes to see discerns it there. What is done in secret shall be told upon the housetops is one of the words of the all-seeing Master, and that is as sadly true of hidden sins as it is joyfully true of hidden victories. Our hidden sins tell upon what we are, and what we are is the secret of our influence. It is the life that is lived beyond the gaze of men that determines a man's value at the last. Therefore be watchful. There is an audience always. There are eyes that go to and fro throughout the earth. In the loneliness of the crowd is One who sees, and our glad assurance is—He sees to save.

O Lord, Thou hast deceived me, and I was
deceived (Jer. 20:7).

29

The Deceptions of God

W hen Jeremiah cried this cry, he had been a prophet for some
twenty years. Everything was dark and ominous for him; he was set
in the stocks as a troubler of Israel. He looked back to the day when
he was called, and he remembered all that had happened to him
since. He thought of the glorious promises God had made him, and
he compared them with all he had suffered in the years. "I will be
with thee to deliver thee," God had said, yet here he was a prisoner
in the stocks. "I will make thy word a word of power," God had
said, yet his word had been tossed aside and laughed to scorn. It is
little wonder that the prophet, plunged in the deepest melancholy
and haunted by an overwhelming sense of failure, should have
cried, "O Lord, Thou hast deceived me, and I was deceived." We
know, looking back upon it all, that he was not deceived. Every
promise made him was royally fulfilled. He came through a sea of
troubles safe and sound, and his word is living and powerful to this
day. But the point is that to this great prophet there came an hour
when heaven seemed to cheat him—"O Lord, Thou hast deceived
me, and I was deceived." On that, then, I wish to dwell tonight, and
I shall arrange what I wish to say under these heads: First, there are
times when we are ready to say that God deceives us. Second, there
are loving purposes in what we think deceit.

First, then, there are times when we are ready to say that God deceives us. Think of the ideals of our childhood. It is one of the sweet illusions of the child that father or mother has neither fault nor flaw. The mother may be vain or very worldly, the father without principle, or worse; but not the angels clad in snow-white garments, nor God Himself in the glory of His throne, are more ideally perfect to the child than are the father and the mother in the home. But that illusion cannot always last. There breaks the day of the knowledge of good and evil. Sometime in boyhood or girlhood comes the hour when the character of the parent is revealed. And though that revelation, thank God, is often noble, disclosing worth never discerned before, yet sometimes it is very sore and desolating and sad with the shattering of many a dream. That hour is a very momentous hour, for the disillusionment of youth is full of peril. So much is bound up with the ideals of childhood that when they vanish many a star is darkened. And it is then for the first time in life, not in words but in the language of the heart, that one may have to cry with Jeremiah, "O Lord, Thou hast deceived me, and I was deceived."

Or think again of the deceptions of the senses. If there is one thing that seems above dispute, it is that this earth of ours is fixed and firm. The tides may ebb and flow, the stars may circle, but the earth we dwell on is steadfast and immovable. If there is one thing we would stake our life on, it is that the sun rises in the east, and that in the west, with the flaming ministry of cloud, it sinks out of our ken beyond the hills. If there is one thing that our eyesight tells us, it is that the clouds are fleecy, and that the sky is blue, and that on a frosty night the stars are twinkling. But the day comes when we unlearn all that, We find that we have walked in a vain show. The earth is not still, sunrise is but a name, the heavens are not blue, there is never a star that twinkles. We have been cheated by our eyes since we were born, yet God is the creator of the eye. To most of us such thoughts give small concern, but to some men they suggest the deepest problems. Such cannot look abroad upon the universe without interrogating the divine morality. Hence to these questioners, as to the prophet, come seasons when the heart is prone to cry, "O Lord, Thou hast deceived me, and I was deceived."

Think once again of how God fulfills His promises. We read of the call of Abraham tonight. One thing certain is that when Abraham was called from Ur, he was promised the land of Canaan for his own. That was to be his inheritance—that land of milk and honey; he was to have it and hold it in the name of God, and in that glad hope, which glowed like a star before him, Abraham went out, not knowing whither he went. The strange thing is that to his dying hour Abraham did not own one rod of Palestine. He was a stranger there, dwelling in his tent, and forced to haggle about a grave for Sarah. Yet all these valleys and all these vineclad hills and the green pastures and the rushing watercourses, all these, in the promise which inspired the pilgrimage, had been conveyed to Abraham as his own. It is a signal tribute to the splendor of Abraham's faith that not in his darkest hour did he doubt God. Dimly and slowly through the earthly vision his eyes were opened to a better country. But to men of weaker faith here is the peril, that when a promise is not fulfilled as they expected, they have no eyes for its more glorious accomplishment and think they have been tricked by the Almighty. Such hours are always big with danger; we are so wedded to our anticipations. There is not a harder task in life to learn than that the letter kills and the spirit gives life. So are we tempted, when a promise fails us because we have narrowed it to our interpretation, to cry as the prophet Jeremiah cried, "O Lord, Thou hast deceived me, and I was deceived."

Think once again of how life deceives us. That is a commonplace of poets and philosophers. Across a thousand dramas and a thousand novels might be written, "The vanity of human wishes." Now I believe that this aspect of existence is often morbidly and grossly overstated. Life never can be a pageant of despair to the man who lives it valiantly and well. Still for all that, between the dreams of youth and the actual accomplishment of after days, between the dewy freshness of the morning and the duller sky of the gray afternoon, between these things is such a vast disparity, that men are touched with the sense of being foiled. "The one word that I would write across my life," said Lord Kelvin at a gathering across the way[1] some years ago—"the one word that would describe my life is failure." That is the season when this cry is born, the cry of Jeremiah in the stocks. It is when men compare all that the years have brought with the glad and golden promise of the morning. It is then that they are tempted, not in bitterness but in the melancholy which Jeremiah knew so well, to cry, "O Lord, if *this* be life, Thou hast deceived me, and I was deceived."

---

1. At the University of Glasgow, from which Wellington Church is separated by an avenue. William Thomson, 1st Baron of Kelvin (1824–1907), English physicist and mathematician.

Then think for a moment of the Christian calling: "Come unto Me, and I will give you rest." And we come, for we are weary and it is rest we want, and immediately we are summoned out to war. "Fight the good fight of faith; put on thine armor; show thyself a good soldier of Christ Jesus"—but, Lord, it was rest we came for, and not war. And then we read that the kingdom of God is peace, and we press through the gates of it to share that peace, only to find ourselves beset with cravings for that which here we shall never realize. Have we been tricked, then, into accepting Christ? Let apostles and saints and martyrs answer that. There is not a promise in the whole New Testament but is "yea and amen in Jesus Christ." Only it is so different from what we dreamed, so contrary to our first and fond imaginings; there are such depths in its conquering simplicity, such unexpected sternness in its joy, that sometimes we could cry with Jeremiah, "O Lord, Thou hast deceived me, and I was deceived."

Now a word or two upon our second thought: there are loving purposes in this so-called deception. Let me direct your minds to some of these.

Sometimes this is one of the ways of God for strengthening and educating character. He leaves us, not because He is false nor because He has broken the promise of His help, but because, like a mother with her little child, He is teaching us to stand upon our feet.[2] Had Jeremiah been ringed around with strength, he never would have cried this bitter cry. Had his message been instantly and heartily received, he never would have thus complained of God. But was it not the baffling of his hopes, and the world of sorrows he was called to bear, that revealed his depth and tenderness of character and made him so true a forerunner of Christ? It is not always the crowning we expect that is our richest blessing from the throne. Things which we never looked for in the morning may be the love of heaven in disguise. And we think it strange, for it is not what we wished for—O Lord, can it be You have deceived us?—but at last we find, as Jeremiah did, how much we owe to a love that seemed to fail.

Again, it is one of God's ways to make us happy, and God is at infinite pains to make us happy. There are dreams so sweet that He will not rudely awaken us; the time for that is coming by and by. Where would the happiness of childhood be, if childhood knew

---

2. Ezekiel 2:1

what one day must be learned? Where would be the heart to face life's battle, if the sweet illusions of youth could be destroyed? But all the warnings of the saints and sages will never crush the dreams of one-and-twenty, and I want you to believe God means it so. Our hopes are not less ministers of happiness because they may never be fully realized. Our memories are not less sweet and tender because we know that the past was never so. And the blue sky will always be a joy, and sunrise and sunset always will be beautiful, although we know that sunrise is a phantasm and sunset but an illusion of the eye. It is true that we all walk in a vain show, but remember it is not all the truth. The show is God's, and it is so arranged that it may make us happy as we watch it. For God is not only the divine artificer, He is also the divine artist of the universe, whose picture is not less true because it charms us by what it seems no less than by what it is.

Once more, it is one of God's ways to make us valiant and to stir and rouse us to our best endeavor. I think, for example, of that first hope of Christendom, that the second coming of the Lord was near at hand. "This generation shall not pass until all things are fulfilled"; "We which remain until the coming of the Lord"—that was the bright and burning expectation that shone in the heaven of the early church. But the years passed and Jesus did not come. There was no call of the trumpet; the sky overhead was brass; until some, deadened by the delay, began to murmur, "Thou hast deceived us, and we were deceived." We know today that they were not deceived, for Christ was coming though they knew it not. But tell me, without that burning hope do you think they could ever have suffered and been strong? They were mighty to dare, mighty to do and die, mighty to rise to the best and face the worst, because they lived on the margins of eternity. So does God strengthen us by what He hides not less divinely than by what He shows. He drapes the future, that might unnerve our arm, under a curtain inscribed with "Maranatha." Until at last the hope that cheered us on merges, when the toil and task are over, into a vision that has larger issues than we had dreamed of in the day of strain.

Then lastly, this so-called deception is one of the ways of God to lead us on. There is a beautiful story of Dr. John Brown (author of the precious *Rab and His Friends*), how once, when out walking with some children, he found the little folk growing very weary. He might have scolded them, but he did not do that. He might have made promises, but he did not do that. He went to the thicket and cut half a dozen switches and made the children mount them for their horses. Then they rode home on switch-back, so to speak, and I warrant you never were more mettled[3] steeds; for the children, beguiled by the wise and gentle stratagem, quite forgot how weary they had been. Do you think that Israel would ever have left Egypt had they not been beguiled by love upon their journey? Do you think that we would ever have the heart to travel if we were not beset by stratagems of mercy? So does God lead us through the ideals of childhood and the hopes of youth and the letter of the promise until at last the husk is broken in our grasp, and we find with a strange joy the hidden kernel. Our earthly father may be no longer perfect, but now we have a Father in the heavens. Our hopes of early manhood pass away, but a hope abides that cannot lose its glory. The life that was full of promise becomes rent and torn, only to give gleams of life eternal. "Thou hast deceived us, and we were deceived"—there are times when we are tempted to say that; but we shall find, if we only trust and wait until the day break and the shadows flee away, that what in our ignorance we called deceit was nought but the ingenuity of love.

---

3. spirited

We beseech you . . . that ye study to be
quiet, and to do your own business
(1 Thess. 4:11).

30

The Ambition of Quietness

The church at Thessalonica, to which Paul wrote the letter, was
in an unsettled and distracted state. The gospel had come to it in
such reality that it was tempted to be untrue to duty. We have all
known how a city is excited when tidings are brought to it of some
great victory. The streets are thronged, the schoolboys get a holiday,
men find it hard to persist in the day's drudgery. It was with somewhat of the same intensity of impress, with its consequent unsettlement and stir, that the news of the risen Christ came to this city.
Bosomed in that news, too, was the assurance that the Christ who
had risen was soon to come again. However Paul's views may have
changed in later years, when he wrote this letter that was his firm
belief. And you may be sure that what Paul believed he taught, so
that (as you may see on every page here) the Thessalonians were
filled with a great joy that in a little while Christ would come again.
It was that which made them so troubled when one died, for they
feared he had missed the glory of Christ's coming. It was that
which made it very hard to labor, for who could tell but that Christ
might come that day. And as with most excitement there is a certain
restlessness, and an unloosing of the tongue in noisy speech, so

among the Christians of this early church there would doubtless be
some lack of self-restraint. It was to combat that almost inevitable
temper that Paul gave the counsels of our verse. He was not speaking to philosophic students. He was speaking to handicraftsmen,
many of them weavers. And he said, "Make it your ambition to be
quiet, and to do your own work as we commanded you, that you
may walk honorably toward them who are without."

Now the truth which unites the clauses of our text is that quietness is needed for true work. Study to be quiet and to do your
business; you will never do the one without the other. In a measure
that is true of outward quiet, at least when we reach the higher kinds
of labor. The thinker, the student, the poet cannot work when they
are tortured by perpetual din. Every man who is earnest about the
highest work makes it his ambition to be quiet. Is he an artist? he
seeks a quiet studio. Is he a thinker? he seeks a quiet study. The best
of the Waverley novels[1] were all written in the dewy stillness of the
early morning and before the locust-bands that swarmed to Abbots-
ford put quietness out of the question for Sir Walter. Of course there
is a certain type of man that is largely impervious to outward tumult. Mr. Gladstone[2] could read and write in Downing Street[3] in
total oblivion of the marching of the Horse Guards. But that does
not mean that he did not require quietude; it means that he could
command an inward quietude and that he was master of such concentration as visits most of us only in rare moments. It is the duty of
every man who does the higher work to make it his ambition to be
quiet. If he is called to his task by the clear will of God, he must
strive for the right conditions for his task. And to me it is wonderful
how in this age of din, and when the uproar of life is so all-
penetrating—how work that is fine and delicate and beautiful man-
ages to get itself fulfilled at all.

But the words of our text have a far deeper meaning than can
ever be exhausted by quietness of circumstances. They tell us that
the best work is never possible unless there be a quietness of the
heart. When a man is inwardly racked and torn and restless, you can
very often tell it on his face. But if it only told on his face it would
be little; the pity is that it tells upon his work. No matter how
humble a man's task may be, no matter how ordinary and

---

1. The Waverly novels written by Sir Walter Scott.
2. William Ewart Gladstone (1809–1898), British statesman and prime minister.
3. home of the British prime minister

uninteresting, he cannot set himself to do it faithfully without imprinting his very being on it; and if within the man there be no peace but a surging of excitement or unrest, that inward tumult will tell on all his toil and subtly influence everything he does. It is one of the legends of our Savior's childhood that in Joseph's workshop He was a perfect worker. If He made a plow, it was a faultless plow. If He made a toy, there was not a flaw in it. It is only a legend, and yet, like every legend, it leans for its secret of beauty on a truth, and the truth is that here was perfect peace, and perfect peace produced the perfect work. Study to be quiet and to do thy business. Make it your ambition to have a heart at leisure. Without that there is no perfecting of fellowship, and without it no perfecting of toil.

Think, for example, of the disquiet of despondency; does not that tangle all that we put our hand to? Let a man be plunged into profound despondency, and every blow of his hammer is affected. There come to all of us, in spite of resolve and prayer, hours when the zest and charm of things depart; hours when there is no edge on any feeling and when all the expanse is desolate and parched; hours when a man is unutterably wretched and when a woman for one kindly word will weep. It may be that there is sin deep down in that, or it may be that the frame is overtaxed; or that melancholy mood may come, we know not how, in the very season when we looked for gladness; but coming, with its profound unsettlement, it steals the joy from everything we do and spreads itself like some benumbing poison through the living tissue of our work. The slightest task weighs heavily upon us, and difficulties are magnified a thousand fold; things that yesterday we could have faced with ease seem to be insurmountable today; but it is not things which have changed, it is ourselves; we are grown nerveless in a deep disquiet. We cannot throw ourselves upon our task with joy, for we have lost the heart at leisure from itself.

The same is true of the unrest of the passions; work becomes drudgery in their disquiet. Let a man be secretly tossed by any passion, and how irksome grows the routine of common days! It is hard to bend the head over one's books when the voices of the sweet world begin to call. It is hard to serve in warehouse and in shop when the heart is torn and tortured with anxiety. It is hard to take up the tasks of life again and to be courteous and wholehearted and unselfish, when the waves of a recent and overwhelming sorrow are breaking and beating still upon the shore. Luther used to say about his preaching that he never could preach except when he was angry. Perhaps there are some of us who would be better preachers were we a little more angry, now and then. But the anger that kindles a man's powers is rare, and the anger that degrades or darkens them is common. The angry man is generally wrong, and when a man is wrong his work is never right. The best work of a school is never done in the tumultuous days before vacation. The best work of a clerk is never done in the whirling season when he is in love. Why, when a domestic servant grows forgetful and handles things in an absent-minded way, does not her kindly mistress smile and say, "Mary must be in love"? I protest against exciting books and plays. I protest against exciting games and dances. And I protest against them because their net result is to make life not easier but harder. For nine-tenths of an honest life is toil, and toil demands a certain noble quietude, a settlement of spirit which is hard to keep and perilously easy to destroy. It is no chance that this exciting age should be an age of much disgraceful workmanship. I hear on every hand today bitter complaints of the rarity of true and faithful service. And I say no wonder, when the ambition of the day is at every cost to be excited. The day of faithful work will come again, but only when men study to be quiet.

Again, the need of inward quiet for toil is seen in the working of an uneasy conscience. Are we not tempted to think of a guilty conscience as something a little apart from daily life; something which has to do with a great God and is therefore remote from the traffic of the hour? I want you to learn there is not a thing you do, not a task or duty you can set your hand to, which is not adversely and evilly affected, if at the back of all there be an unquiet conscience. You may be a student working at your classes or a servant busied in the sunless kitchen; you may have to control a mighty business, or in that business you may be the humblest clerk; but whatever your work is, a conscience void of peace will tell upon and influence that work and interpenetrate it all so surely, that to its finest fiber it will feel your guilt. We smile a little today at the great text, "Be sure your sin will find you out." We have grown so liberal and so enlightened that we can jest at twilight superstitions. But if one thing is certain, it is that that text is true, and that every sin we have cherished finds us out and finds us out, not by the trump of God, but by the resistless evolving of its consequence. Some find us out, long after, in our bodies. Some in the bosom of our pleasant homes. Some lie asleep until we are near our victory, and then they waken and snatch away the laurel. But always, in the temper of our work, in the tone and strength of it, and in its joy and quality, there is more than the impress of our brain and hand, there is also the impress of our conscience. Conscience doth make cowards of us all, and if a man be a coward, his work is sure to show it. There must be peace within and the joy that comes from peace, if the meanest task is to be nobly done. And that is why the Gospel of Christ Jesus, which through the precious blood brings peace of conscience, has given the world a new ideal of toil and enriched the humblest toiler with new joy. Study to be quiet, then, and do your business. Make it your ambition to have the rest of Christ. A heart tumultuous and hot and restless is a sorry comrade for the leaden days. But a heart at peace and passions in subjection and a conscience void of offense toward God and man will send a man wholeheartedly to duty and help to make that duty a delight.

Let us lay aside every weight, and the sin which doth so easily beset us . . . looking unto Jesus (Heb. 12:1–2).

31

On Weights

When the writer speaks of the sin which doth beset us he is not referring to one particular sin. The thought that one sin may be specially perilous is not present to his mind at all. He is thinking of all sin, of sin in its largest compass, and he says of all sin that it easily besets us, which probably means that, like a hampering garment, it clings to us and hinders us from running. Now mark that he does not say, "Let us lay aside our weights, *even* the sins that so easily beset us." He puts an "and" between the words to indicate that the one obstruction may differ from the other. All sins are weights, but all weights are not sins; and both alike have to be laid aside.

A moment's thought ought to make plain to us this great distinction between weights and sins; it is one that vitally concerns our progress. There are some things that everywhere are right, and there are other things that everywhere are wrong. No matter who does them or why they may be done, their relation to the law of God is fixed. They do not take their moral tone from circumstances nor are they relative to a man's place or powers. There are things that are everywhere and always right, and there are things that are everywhere and always wrong. Now could we take every detail of human conduct and place it in one or other of these categories, life would present a very simple problem; but the complexity of life consists in this, that there are acts innumerable which cannot be so classified. There are a thousand things that no man dare call wrong, for they show none of the characters of sin; on the contrary, they may be precious gifts which in other circumstances might be rich in blessing; but if they hinder you when you struggle for the best and burden you so that you run unworthily, then are they weights and must be laid aside.

That this is also the teaching of our Lord is evident from some of His memorable sayings: "If thy right hand offend thee, cut it off"; "If thy right eye offend thee, pluck it out." Is anything sinful in the hand and eye? Are they not instruments and avenues of blessing? Of all the gifts that man has had from heaven there are few that can be matched with hand or eye. In the right hand has waved the sword of freedom. In the right hand has been grasped the pen of genius. By the right hand is wrought that common toil that sets a hundred temptations at defiance—yet "if thy right hand offend thee, cut it off; if thy right eye offend thee, pluck it out." Do not misinterpret that deep word of Jesus. He spoke as a poet speaks, who through the concrete has visions of abstract and universal truth. He meant that even the choicest of our blessings may be so twisted and turned into a snare that a man may have to say, "This is a weight for me," and with swiftness of farewell, lay it aside.

Of course we shall remember that there are certain weights which are a help and not a hindrance to our progress. They impart a certain momentum to the character and carry a man through obstacles victoriously. There are men who by nature are light-weights with little chance, in this hard world, of prospering; and God has to steady them with burdens sometimes, if they are to run with patience the race that is set before them. I should not like to travel in a train if I were told that it was light as match-wood. I should not like to put to sea in a great steamer if I were informed there was no ballast in her. When there are curves to be taken or storms to be encountered, when the way is beset with obstacles or perils, you need a certain weight to ensure safety, and you need a certain weight to give you speed. I have no doubt that this is the explanation of many of the weights that we must carry. They steady and ballast us; they give us our momentum as we drive ahead through the tempestuous sea. Life might be lighter and merrier if we lacked them; but, after all, there are better things than merriment. It is a real weight to a young man, sometimes, that he has to support an aged relative. There is much that he craves for which he can never get so long as that burden at home is on his shoulders. But has not that burden made a man of him—made him strenuous and serious and earnest? He might have run his race with brilliance otherwise, but he runs it with patience now, and that is better. There are few weights like the weight at a father's heart when his little and well-beloved child falls sick. It is with him when he wakens in the morning, and it hangs about him heavily all day. But how often does it touch his heart with tenderness and call in his roving and unworthy passion and make him vow to be a better father and bring him back to the secrecy of prayer. There are weights that are helps, then, and not to be cast aside. They are of God's appointing and must be carried bravely. There are burdens which we know in our conscience to be hindrances; but there are others which in the eyes of God are blest.

Nor is this a matter in which one who is wise will ever dare to pass judgment on another. We can tell as the days go by what are weights to us; we can never tell what are weights to other men. The thing that vexes us at every turn and causes us wearily to sigh for freedom may to another man be a good gift of God that sends him singing and happy on his journey. If you were to clothe a modern cavalry officer in the chain armor of a medieval knight, it would be almost insupportable to him and would prove itself an intolerable weight. But the knight himself, "pricking o'er the plain,"[1] or dashing into combat with the Saracen,[2] was safe and strong when girded with that mail. There are few who could handle the sword of Sir William Wallace;[3] it is so massive, and of such a weight; yet in the hand of Wallace it used to flash like lightning—to him it was not a burden but a joy. Never, then, judge others in such matters and never permit others to judge you. In things indifferent it is a sign of weakness to be quickly influenced by the report of others. The personal test which one should boldly use when he is doubtful of any act or habit is to ask himself, "Is this a help or hindrance in the patient running of the race?" If he can honestly say it is a help, then probably it were cowardice to reject it. There are times when it is

---

1. From "To Sir Christopher Halton" by Edmund Spenser (1552?–1599), English poet.

2. A Muslim, especially if mentioned in connection with the Crusades.

3. Sir William Wallace (1272?–1305), Scottish military leader and patriot.

the duty of a Christian to insist bravely upon his Christian liberty. But if his conscience tells him that it is a hindrance, then let him summon his manhood and dismiss it, though it should take the sunshine from the morning and silence all the singing of the birds.

Sometimes, too, these things that we call weights are of the most insignificant and trifling kind. They are like the weights beside a chemist's scales, so tiny as hardly to be visible. I wonder what a thorn would turn the scale at? There would be a good many thousands to the pound. Caught in the fleece of a sheep upon the hills, it would not hinder it from freest movement. But plunged in the flesh of a great saint like Paul, it hampers and retards at every turn, until even the thorn for Paul becomes a weight and drives him in entreaty to the Throne. I think there are few things sadder in the world than the trifling nature of much that hinders men. There are thousands who are within an ace of running well, with one thing only between them and freedom. And that is often such a little thing—such a trifle, such an insignificancy—that the pity is that a man should be so near and yet, from the triumph of it all, so far.[4] If men were ruined only by great sins, there would be a tragic splendor in existence. No one can study a tragedy of Shakespeare without being purified thereby at heart. But men are not only ruined by great sins; they are also beaten in the race by little weights, and it is just the relative lightness of the weight that is the pity of a thousand lives. If that should describe your case, my brother, I plead with you to lay aside that weight. It may be hard; in deed it is often harder to lay aside the little than the great one. Others may smile at you, not grasping what it means; they say, "What does it matter, it is such a trifle?" But in the sight of heaven and at the bar of conscience, you know it is keeping you from running well.

But someone will say to me, "That is good advice, but I have had as good advice before. It is not advice I want, but it is power to do it, for I have tried a dozen times and failed." Well, I believe you—I have had that experience; but never since I saw what this text meant. "Lay aside every weight, *looking unto Jesus*"—there is the open secret of success. Depend upon it, if you look at the weight only, you will never have the heart to lay it down. It will never seem to you so fixed and firm as in the hour you are determined to

4. "Oh the little more, and how much it is!
   And the little less, and what worlds away!"
   Browning, *By the Fire-side*, p. 39.

reject it. And once rejected, all that you had against it will be so overborne in wild desire that with greedy hands you will draw it back again to find it doubly sweet because forsworn. That is the certain path toward night and tears, for every such failure leaves the conscience poorer. The saddest hour is not when a man is beaten; it is when he says, "O God, this is impossible"; but there is no such hour, even for the weakest, if he will only act as this text bids him, and "lay aside, looking unto Jesus." Keep your gaze fixed on Jesus Christ the crucified. Direct every power of your heart toward Him. Believe in His nearness, His love, His mighty power—He carried the weight of the world's guilt triumphantly. It is wonderful, if one will but do that, how the weight that seemed to be soldered will grow movable, so that a man this very night may cast it from him and waken in the morning—free!

And now I have just one other word to say. It is about these weights which we cannot lay aside. It is about these things which really may be hindrances, and which yet we dare not or cannot put away. It may be perhaps some bodily defect. It may be some relationship at home. It may be something connected with our business. It may be the result of folly long ago; and today it hangs about us like a weight, and we know we shall never lose it until the grave. Such things we cannot or dare not lay aside. What then—must they always and to the end be weights? Ah, whether a thing shall be a weight or not depends enormously on how we carry it. Suppose you take a truckload of steel plates and empty these steel plates into the sea. They sink immediately. They are far too heavy a weight to be borne by the yielding and never-resting ocean. But fashion a thousand of such plates into a vessel; hammer and rivet them into a ship of steel; and the ocean will bear them as she would an almond branch and never feel that weight upon her bosom. It is not the thing itself that is the weight; far more often it is the way we carry it. If we be selfish and loveless and out of touch with God, the very grasshopper may be a burden. But if we believe, if we have hope and charity, if we trust in the love of God and look to Jesus, these weights, which we cannot lay aside, will become light just because carried well.

Scripture Index